NORMA
in Full Score

NORMA

in Full Score

Vincenzo Bellini

DOVER PUBLICATIONS, INC.
New York

Copyright

Copyright © 1994 by Dover Publications, Inc.
All rights reserved under Pan American and International Copyright Conventions.

Published in Canada by General Publishing Company, Ltd., 30 Lesmill Road, Don Mills, Toronto, Ontario.

Published in the United Kingdom by Constable and Company, Ltd., 3 The Lanchesters, 162–164 Fulham Palace Road, London W6 9ER.

Bibliographical Note

This Dover edition, first published in 1994, is an unabridged republication of a standard edition. New lists of characters and instruments and a new table of contents have been added, and a few minor omissions in the score have been corrected.

We are grateful to The George Sherman Dickinson Music Library, Vassar College, for the loan of the score.

Library of Congress Cataloging-in-Publication Data

Bellini, Vincenzo, 1801–1835.
    Norma / Vincenzo Bellini ; [libretto by Felice Romani, based on a tragedy by Alexandre Soumet].—In full score.
       1 score.
       Opera in two acts; Italian words.
       Reprint. Originally published: Milano ; New York : G. Ricordi, c1915.
       ISBN 0-486-27970-7 (pbk.)
    1. Operas—Scores.   I. Romani, Felice, 1788–1865.   II. Soumet, Alexandre, 1788–1845. Norma.   III. Title.
M1500.B44N6   1994   93-46335
                                                                                                  CIP
                                                                                                    M

Manufactured in the United States of America
Dover Publications, Inc., 31 East 2nd Street, Mineola, N.Y. 11501

NORMA

Tragic Opera in Two Acts

Libretto by Felice Romani
based on a tragedy by Alexandre Soumet

Music by Vincenzo Bellini

*First performance: La Scala, Milan
26 December 1831*

CHARACTERS

Norma, *High Priestess of the Druids*	Soprano
Adalgisa, *Vestal Virgin*	Soprano
Clotilde, *Norma's confidante*	Mezzo-soprano
Pollione, *Roman military governor in Gaul*	Tenor
Flavio, *centurion, Pollione's friend*	Tenor
Oroveso, *Archdruid, Norma's father*	Bass

Company of Druids, Soldiers,
Norma's Two Children

*Setting: Gaul during the Roman occupation in 1 B.C.,
in the sacred groves and Temple of Irminsul, God of War*

INSTRUMENTATION

2 Flutes [Flauti, Fl.] (and Piccolo [Ottavino, Ott.])
2 Oboes [Oboi, Ob.]
2 Clarinets (in C, B♭) [Clarinetti, Cl. (Do, Si♭)]
2 Bassoons [Fagotti, Fag.]

4 Horns (in C, D, E♭, E, F, G, B♭) [Corni (Do, Re, Mi♭, Mi, Fa, Sol, Si♭)]
2 Trumpets (in C, D, E♭, E, G, B♭) [Trombe, Trbe. (Do, Re, Mi♭, Mi, Sol, Si♭)]
3 Trombones [Tromboni, Trni.]
Cimbasso [Cimb.: *obsolete brass-wind, in the Bass Trombone range*]

Timpani [Timpani, Timp.]
Bass Drum and Cymbals [G. Cassa (G.C.) e Piatti]
Tam-Tam [Tam-Tam]

Harp [Arpa]
Brass Band (*on stage*) [Banda (*sul palco*)]

Violins I, II [Violini, Viol.]
Violas [Viole, Vle.]
Cellos [Violoncelli, Vc.]
Basses [Contrabassi, Cb.]

CONTENTS

Sinfonia 1

Act One

Introductory Chorus and Cavatina (*Oroveso, Chorus*) 33
    Ite sul colle, o Druidi 39 / Dell'aura tua profetica 45

Recitative and Cavatina (*Pollione, Flavio, Chorus*) 65
    Svanir le voci!—Altra ameresti tu? 66 / Meco all'altar di Venere—Quando fra noi terribile 70 / Odi?—Sorta è la Luna—Traman congiure 78 / Me protegge 83 / Vieni... Sorta è la Luna 87

Chorus: Norma viene—In sua man 103

Scena and Cavatina (*Norma, Oroveso, Chorus*) 115
    Sediziöse voci—In pagine di morte 115 / Aria: Casta Diva 123 / Fine al rito 132 / Ah! bello a me ritorna 136 / O giorno 149

Scena (*Adalgisa*): Sgombra è la sacra selva 156

Duet (*Pollione, Adalgisa*) 163
    Eccola!—Pregava 163 / Va, crudele—Sol promessa al dio 166 / Ah! tu pure—Il pensiero—Ciel più puro 174 / Vieni in Roma—Qui, domani—Sì, fedel a te 185

Scena and Duet (*Norma, Clotilde*) 197
    Vanne, e li cela entrambi—Oltre l'usato 203 / Adalgisa!—Alma, costanza 208 / Oh! rimembranza! 212 / Ah! sì, fa core 220

Finale I: Scena and Trio (*Norma, Adalgisa, Pollione*) 227
    Ma di'... l'amato giovane—Il mira 227 / Oh! di qual sei tu vittima 234 / Perfido!—Qual io mi fossi obblio 242 / Vanne, sì 247 / Norma, Norma all'ara! 257

Act Two

Introduction (*Norma, Clotilde*) 265
    Dormono entrambi 268 / I figli uccido! 271

Scena and Duet (*Adalgisa, Norma*) 274
    Me chiami, o Norma? 275 / Deh! con te, con te li prendi 278 / Mira, o Norma 288 / Sì, fino all'ore 296

Chorus: Non partì! 308

Oroveso's Entrance Aria (*Oroveso, Chorus*) 323
    Guerrieri! a voi venirne—Come? le nostre selve 323 / Ah del Tebro 326

Recitative and Chorus (*Norma, Clotilde, Chorus, Oroveso*) 335
    Ei tornerà—o Norma! 336 / Squilla il bronzo del Dio! 341 /
    Norma, che fu?—Ed ira adesso 344 / Guerra, guerra! 349

Scena and Duet (*Oroveso, Norma, Clotilde, Chorus, Pollione*) 361
    Nè compi il rito—Al nostro tempio 361 / Un Romano? 363 /
    Sacrilego nemico 364

Scena (*Norma, Pollione*) 371
    In mia man—Ah! crudele 371 / Tutti. I Romani 376 / Già mi pasco—
    Ch'io mi sveni 379

Final Scena and Aria (*Norma, Chorus, Oroveso, Pollione*) 392
    All'ira vostra nuova vittima 392 / Tu! Norma! 395 / Qual cor
    tradisti 396 / Taci? . . . ne ascolti 410 / Empia!—Tu m'odi 412 /
    Deh! non volerli vittime—Piange! prega! 415 / Vanne al rogo 425

NORMA
in Full Score

NORMA
di
VINCENZO BELLINI
SINFONIA

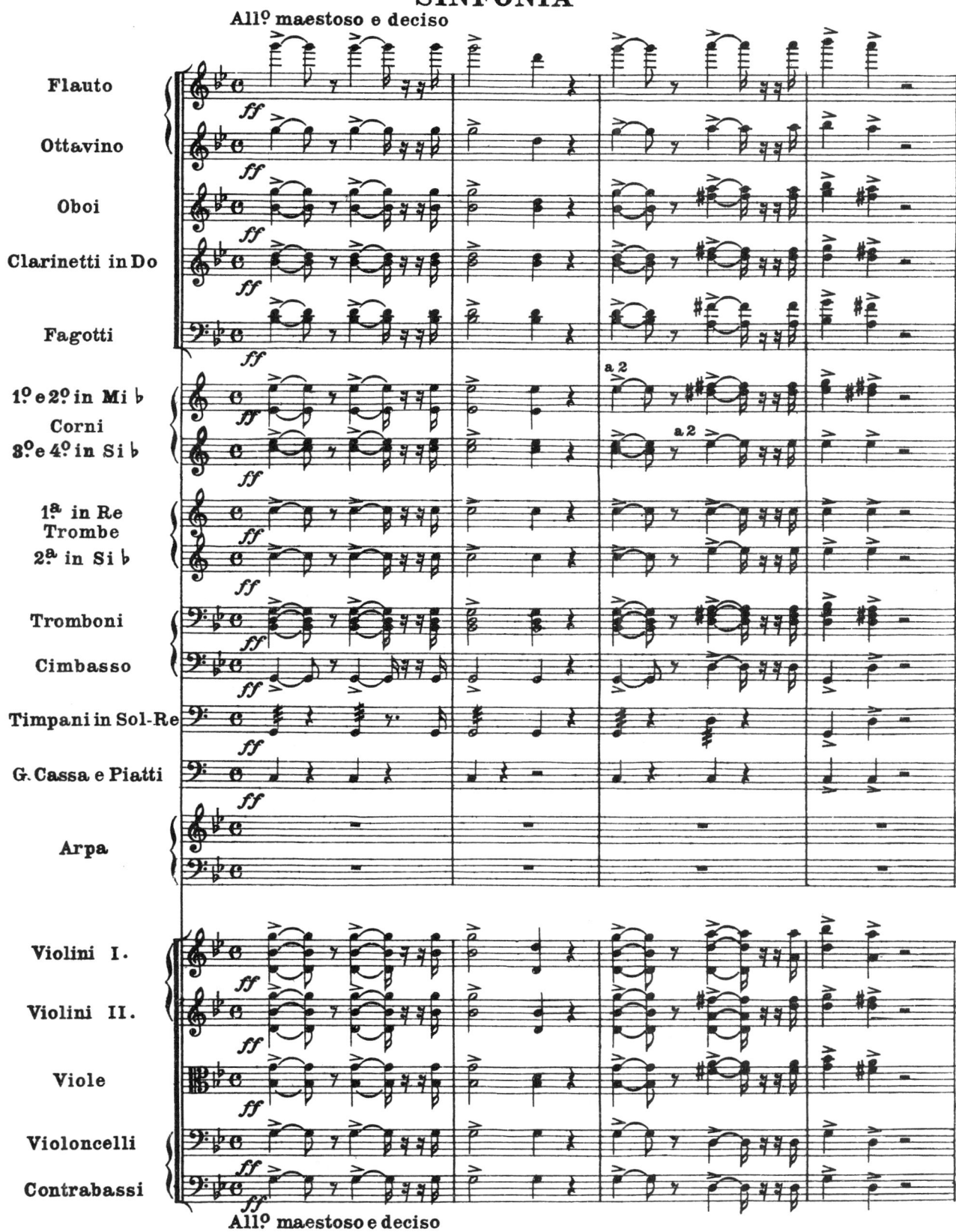

5

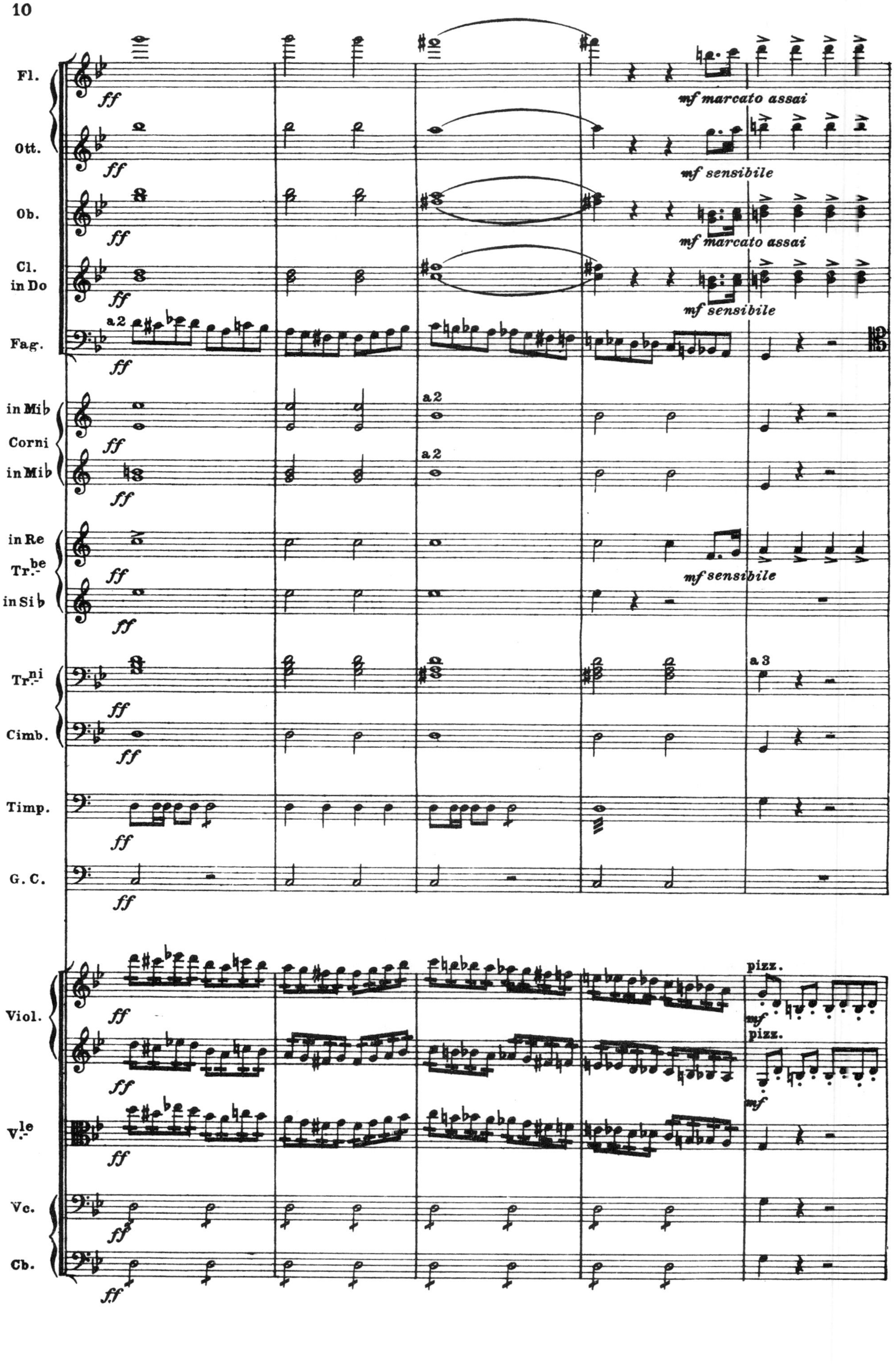
Fl.
Ott.
Ob.
Cl. in Do
Fag.
in Mib
Corni
in Mib
in Re
Tr.be
in Si b
Tr.ni
Cimb.
Timp.
G. C.
Viol.
V.le
Vc.
Cb.
ff
a 2
a 3
mf marcato assai
mf sensibile
mf marcato assai
mf sensibile
mf sensibile
pizz.
pizz.
mf

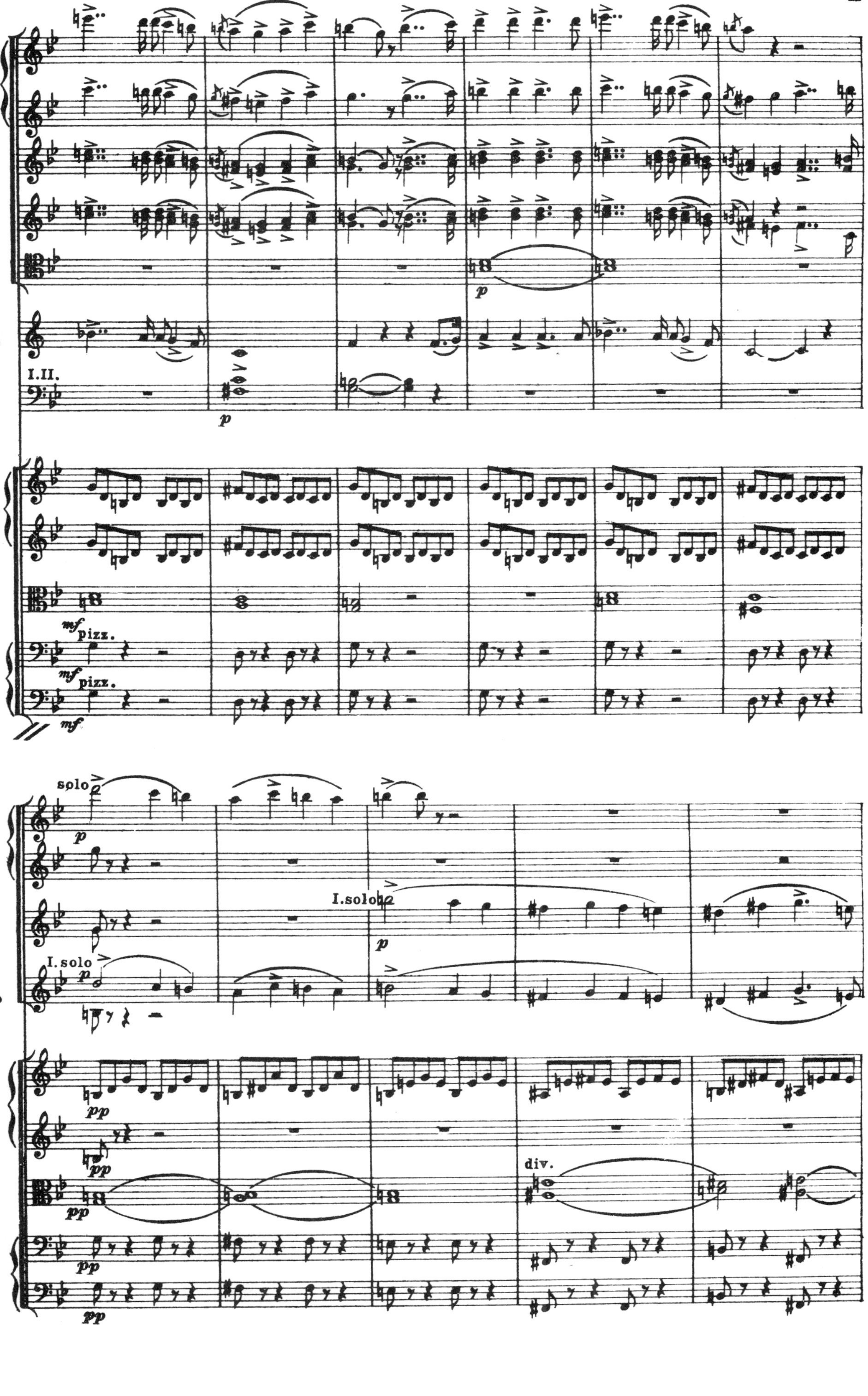
Fl.
Ott.
Ob.
Cl. in Do
Fag.
Tr.-ba in Re
I.II.
Tr.-ni
Viol.
V.-le
Vc.
Cb.
p
mf
pizz.
solo
I.solo
I. solo
pp
div.

12

14

16

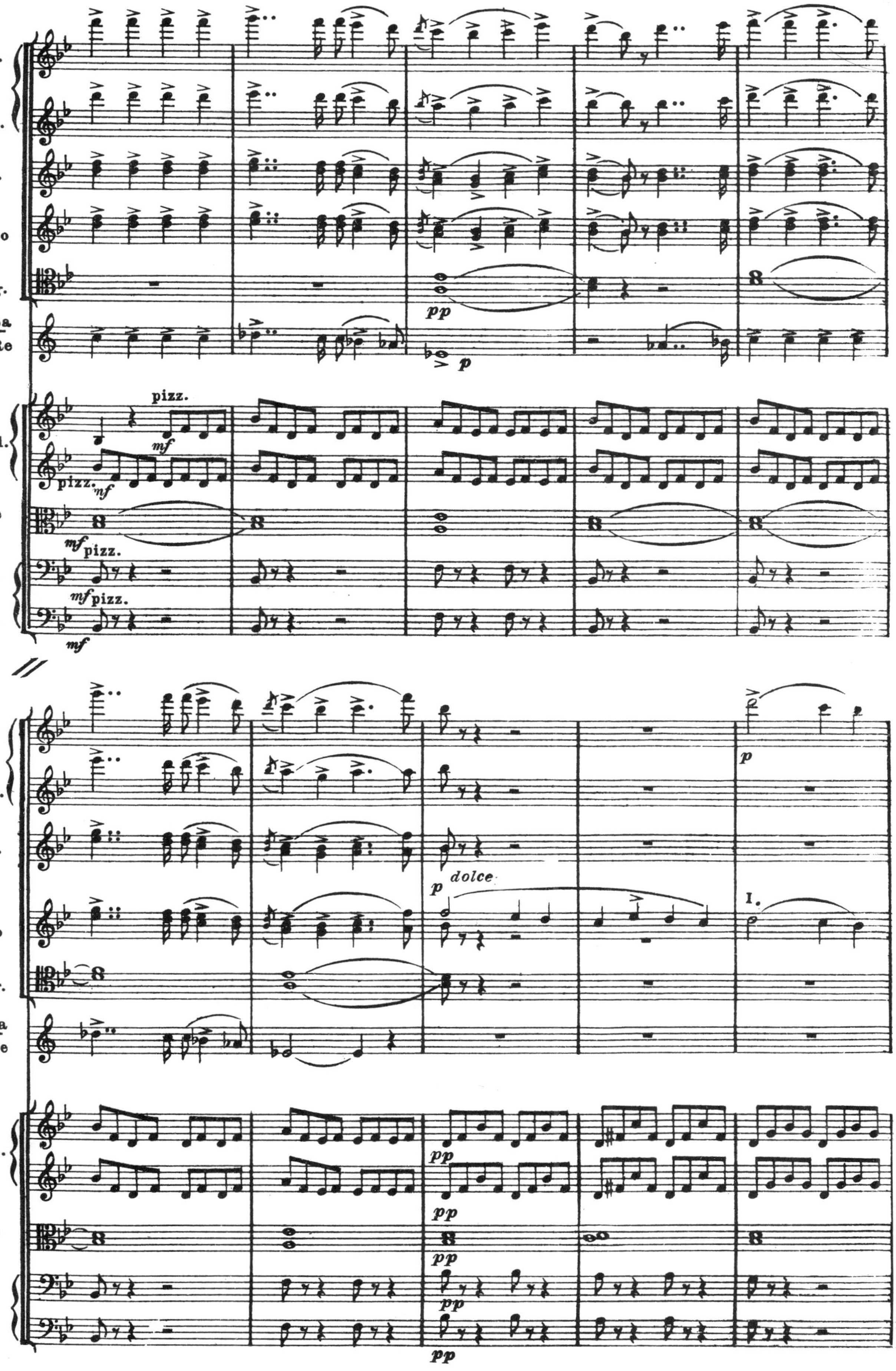
Fl.
Ott.
Ob.
Cl. in Do
Fag.
Tr.ba in Re
Viol.
V.le
Vc.
Cb.
pizz.
mf
pp
p
dolce
I.

18

20

21

22

25

28

30

31

32

ATTO PRIMO
SCENA PRIMA.
Foresta sacra de' Druidi.

In mezzo, la quercia d'Irminsul, al piè della quale vedesi la pietra druidica che serve d'altare. Colli in distanza sparsi di selve. È notte; lontani fuochi trapelano dai boschi.

Al suono di marcia religiosa diffilano le schiere de' Galli, indi la processione dei Druidi. Per ultimo Oroveso coi maggiori Sacerdoti.

Coro d'Introduzione e Cavatina
(OROVESO)

34

36

38

40

42

46

48

50

54

62

Recitativo e Cavatina
(POLLIONE)

SCENA II.

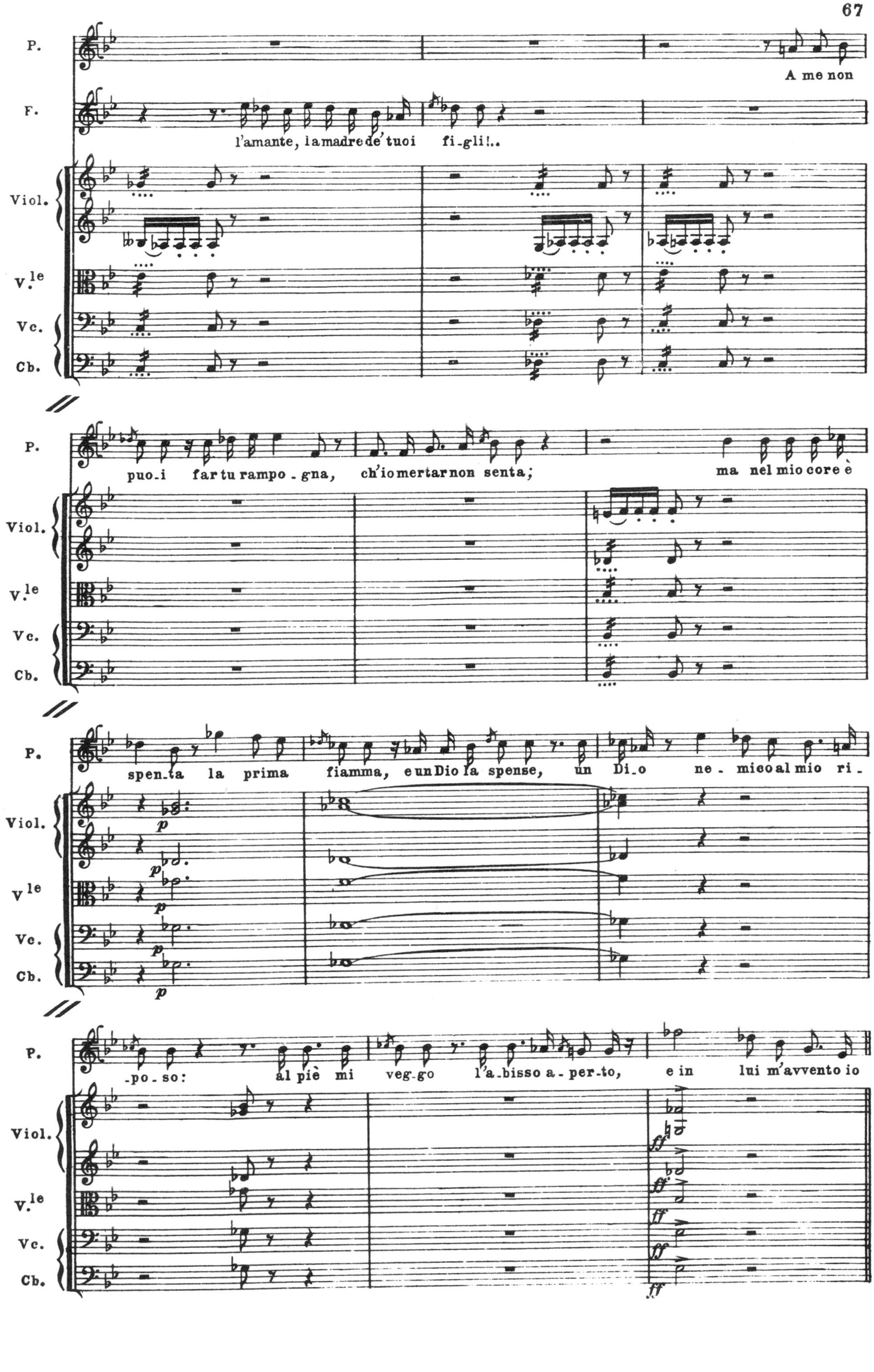
P.
F.
Viol.
V.le
Vc.
Cb.
A me non
l'amante, la madre de' tuoi fi-gli!..
puo-i far tu rampo-gna, ch'io mertar non senta;
ma nel mio core è
spen-ta la prima fiamma, e un Dio la spense, un Di-o ne-mico al mio ri-
-po-so: al piè mi veg-go l'a-bisso a-per-to, e in lui m'avvento io
p
ff

72

-gom - - bra; ca - de sull'a - ra il fol - - gore, d'un vel si co - pre il

82

89

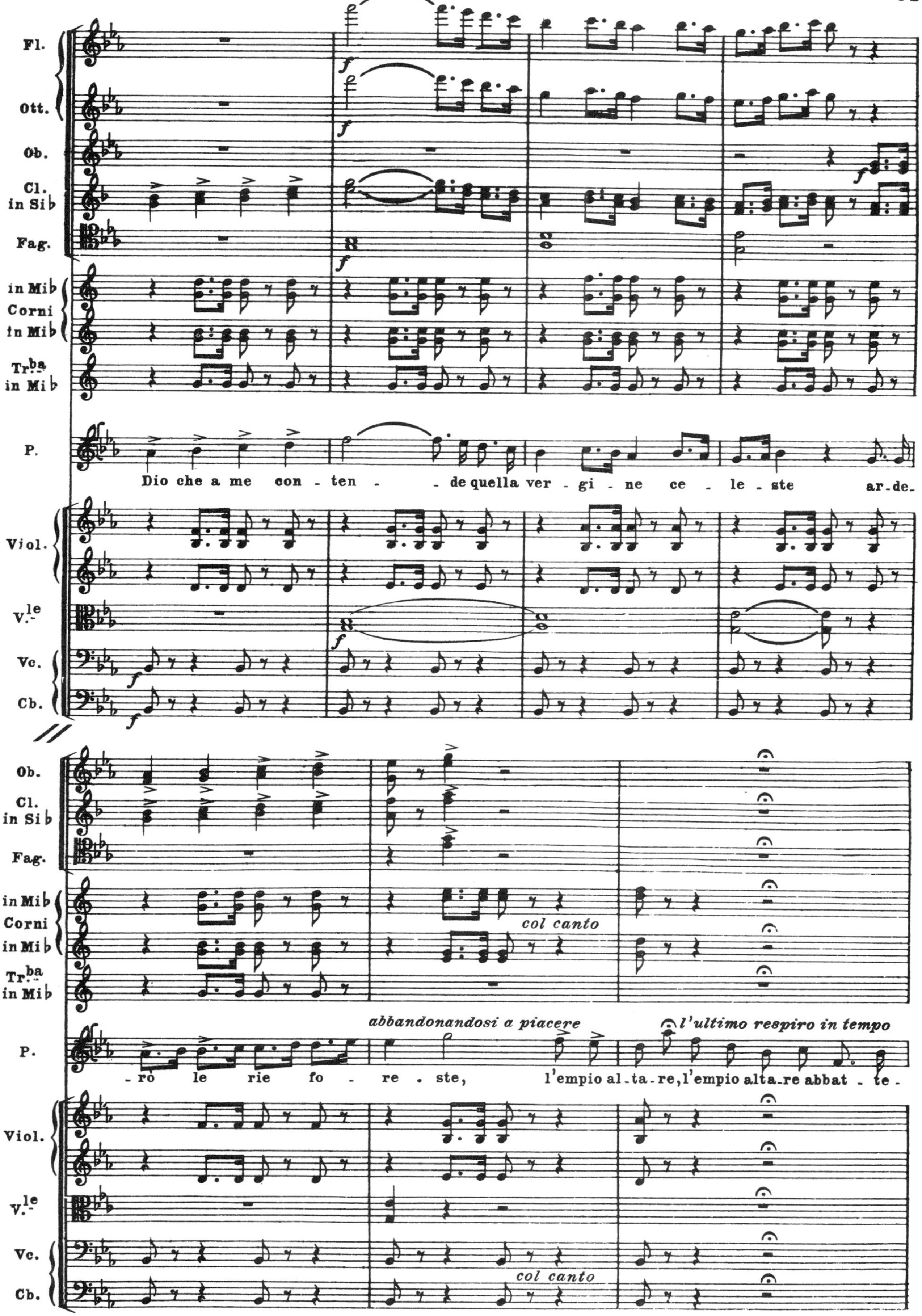
Fl.
Ott.
Ob.
Cl. in Si♭
Fag.
in Mi♭ Corni in Mi♭
Tr.ba in Mi♭
P.
Dio che a me con - ten - - de quella ver - gi - ne ce - le - ste ar-de-
Viol.
V.le
Vc.
Cb.
col canto
abbandonandosi a piacere
l'ultimo respiro in tempo
- rò le rie fo - re - ste, l'empio al-ta-re, l'empio alta-re abbat - te-
col canto

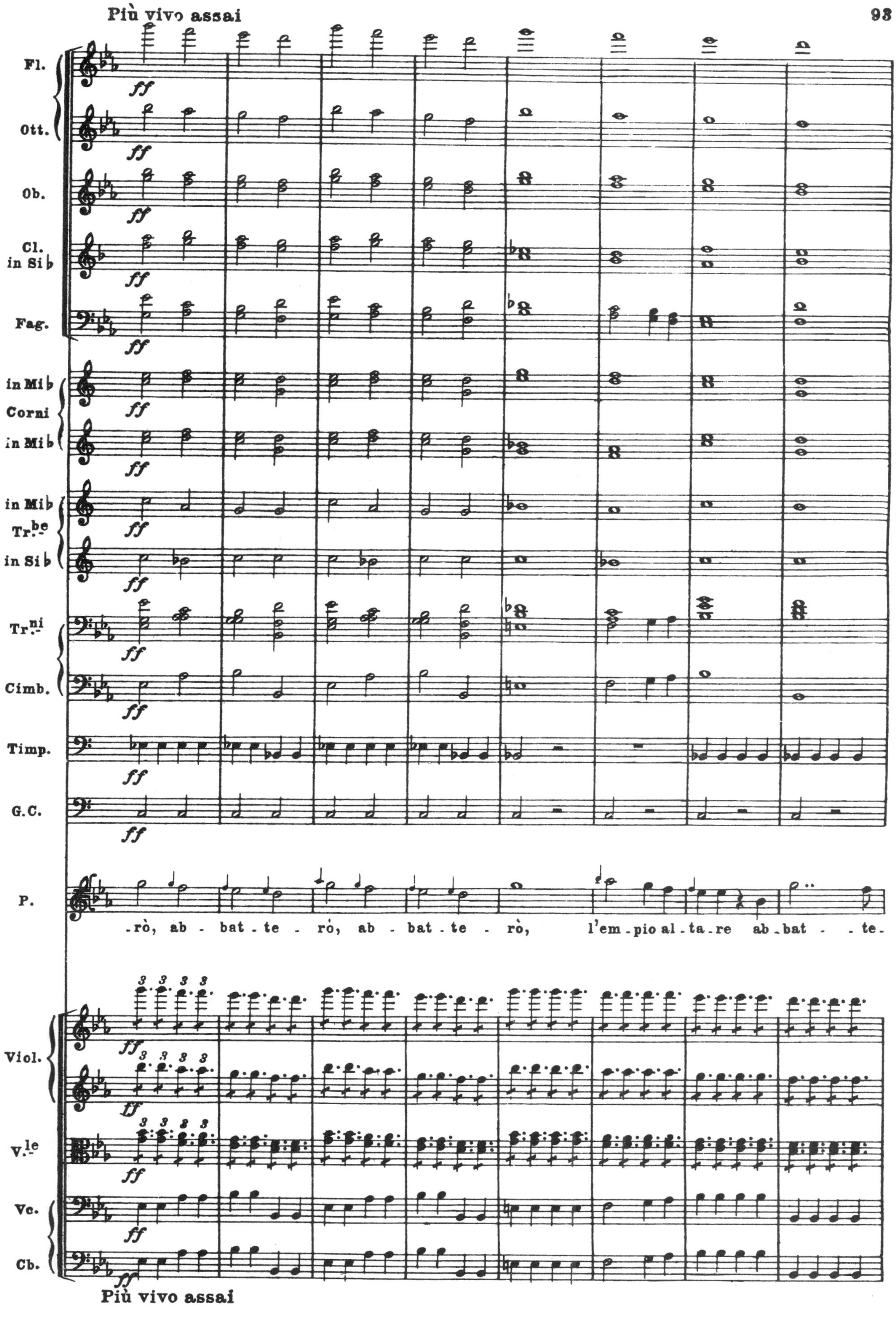
Più vivo assai
Fl.
Ott.
Ob.
Cl. in Si♭
Fag.
in Mi♭
Corni
in Mi♭
in Mi♭
Tr.be
in Si♭
Tr.ni
Cimb.
Timp.
G.C.
P.
-rò, ab - bat - te - rò, ab - bat - te - rò, l'em - pio al - ta - re ab - bat - - te-
Viol.
V.le
Vc.
Cb.
ff
Più vivo assai

94

SCENA III.

Coro

Druidi, dal fondo, Sacerdotesse, Guerrieri, Bardi, Eubagi, Sacrificatori e in mezzo a tutti Oroveso.

100

102

106

108

SCENA IV. Norma in mezzo alle sue ministre. Ha sciolti i capegli, la fronte circondata di una corona di verbena, ed armata la mano d'una falce d'oro. Si colloca sulla pietra druidica, e volge gli occhi d'intorno come ispirata.

Scena e Cavatina
(NORMA)

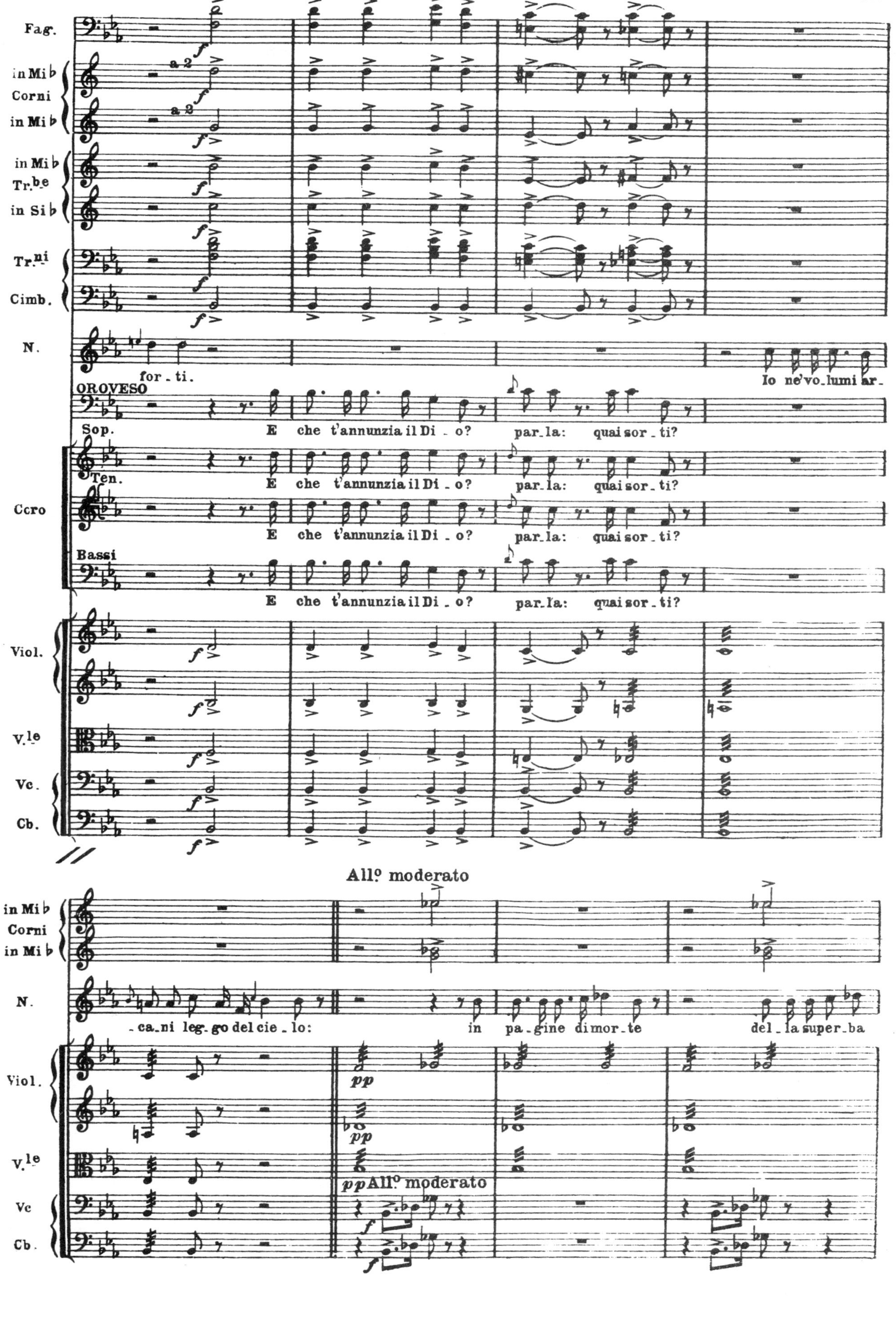
Fag.
Corni in Mi♭
Tr.be in Mi♭ in Si♭
Tr.ni
Cimb.
N.
for - ti.
Io ne'vo-lumi ar-
OROVESO
E che t'annunzia il Di - o? par-la: quai sor - ti?
Sop.
Ten.
Coro
Bassi
Viol.
V.le
Vc.
Cb.
All.o moderato
-ca-ni leg-go del cie-lo: in pa-gine di mor-te del-la super-ba

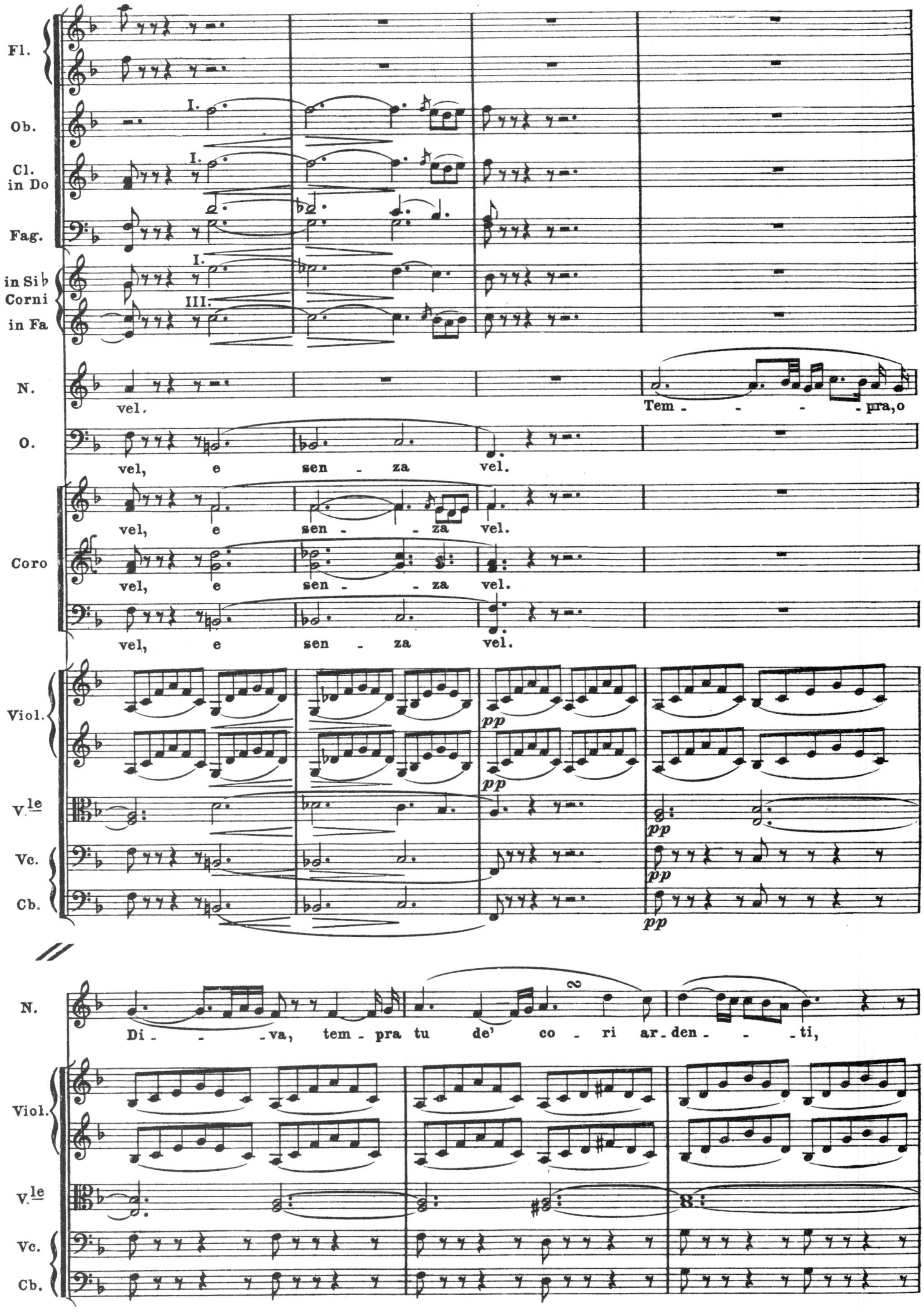

Fl.
Ob.
Cl. in Do
Fag.
in Si♭ Corni in Fa
I.
III.
N.
vel. Tem - - - pra, o
O.
vel, e sen - za vel.
Coro
vel, e sen - - za vel.
vel, e sen - - za vel.
vel, e sen - za vel.
Viol.
V.le
Vc.
Cb.
pp
N.
Di - - va, tem - pra tu de' co - ri ar - den - - ti,
Viol.
V.le
Vc.
Cb.

132

136

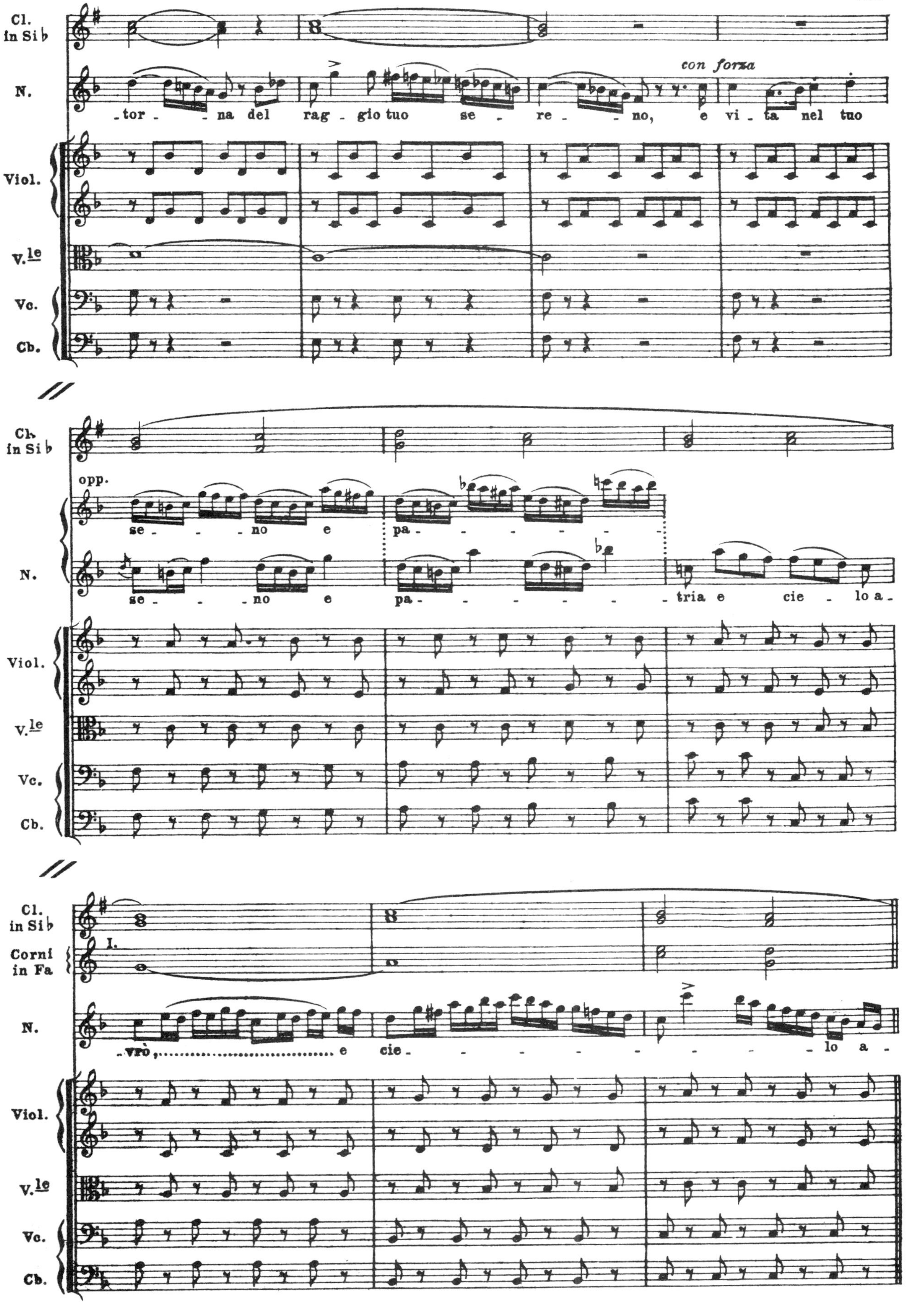
Cl. in Si♭
N.
con forza
tor - na del rag - gio tuo se - re - no, e vi - ta nel tuo
Viol.
V.le
Vc.
Cb.
opp.
se - no e pa -
se - no e pa - tria e cie - lo a -
vrò, e cie - lo a -
Corni in Fa
I.

140

146

151

152

153

154

Scena e Duetto
(ADALGISA E POLLIONE)

SCENA V.

158

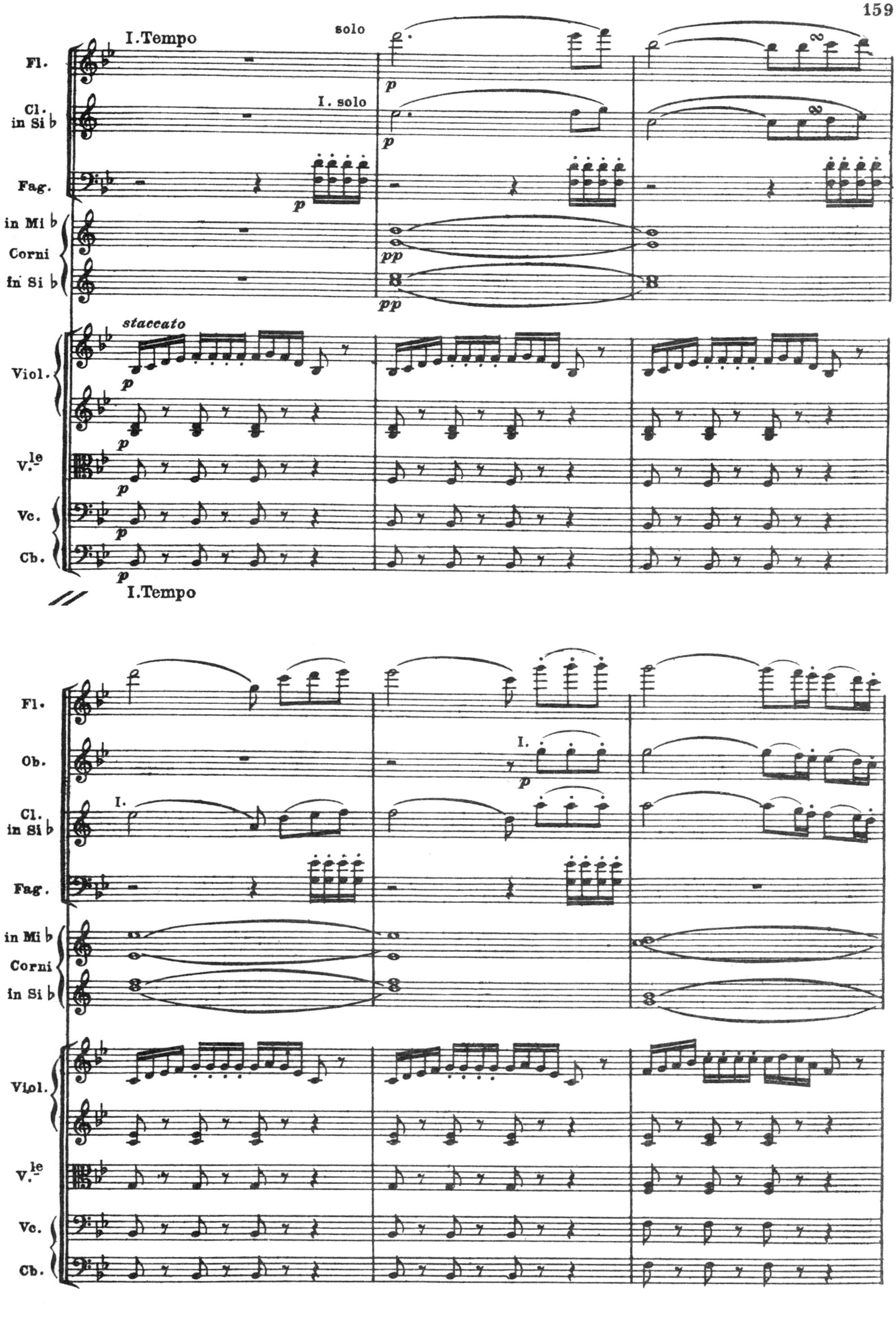
I. Tempo
solo
Fl.
I. solo
Cl. in Si♭
p
Fag.
p
in Mi♭
Corni
in Si♭
pp
staccato
Viol.
p
V.le
Vc.
Cb.
I. Tempo
Ob.
I.

SCENA VI.

Duetto
(ADALGISA E POLLIONE)

co - sti per ch'io mai ri - nun - zi a te,.............per - ch'io........

184

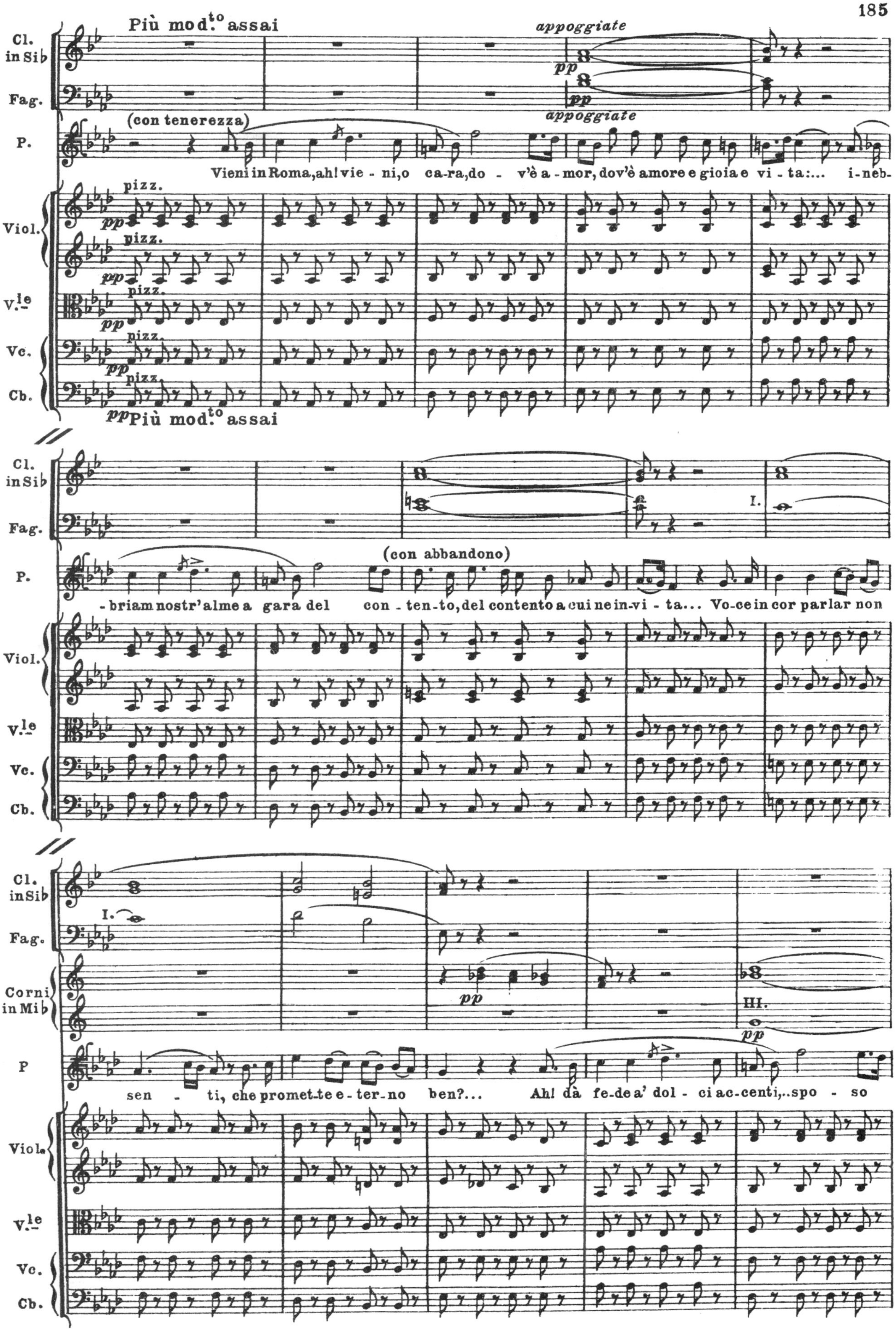
Più mod.to assai
appoggiate
Cl. in Sib
Fag.
P.
(con tenerezza)
Vieni in Roma, ah! vie - ni, o ca-ra, do - v'è a - mor, dov'è amore e gioia e vi - ta:... i-neb-
Viol.
pizz.
pp
V.le
Vc.
Cb.
Più mod.to assai
-briam nostr'alme a gara del con - ten-to, del contento a cui ne in-vi - ta... Vo-ce in cor parlar non
(con abbandono)
I.
Corni in Mib
III.
sen - ti, che promet-te e-ter-no ben?... Ah! dà fe-de a' dol - ci ac-centi,..spo - so

196

SCENA VII.. - Abitazione di Norma. - Norma, Clotilde e due piccoli fanciulli.

Scena
(NORMA e CLOTILDE)

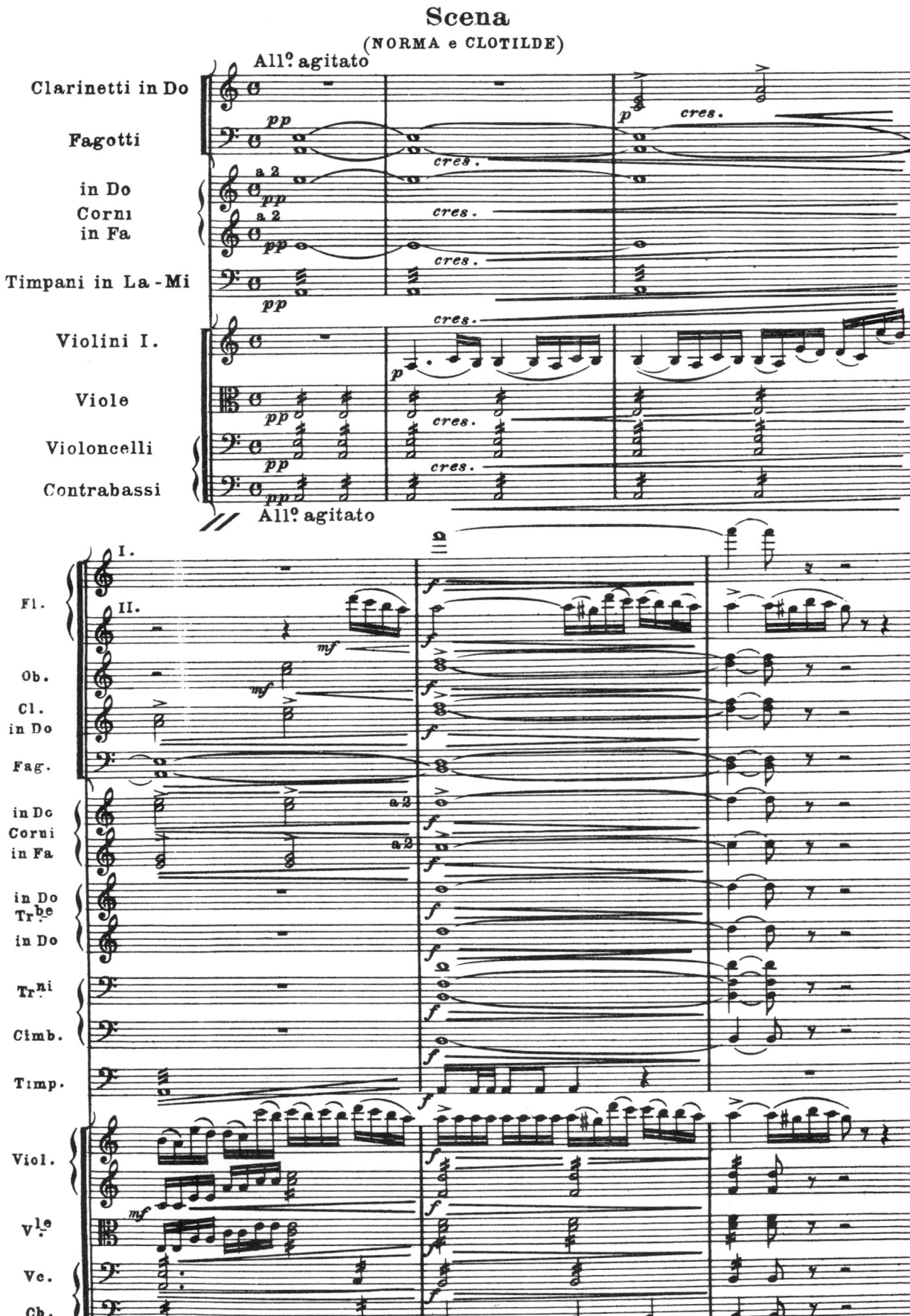

198

199

200

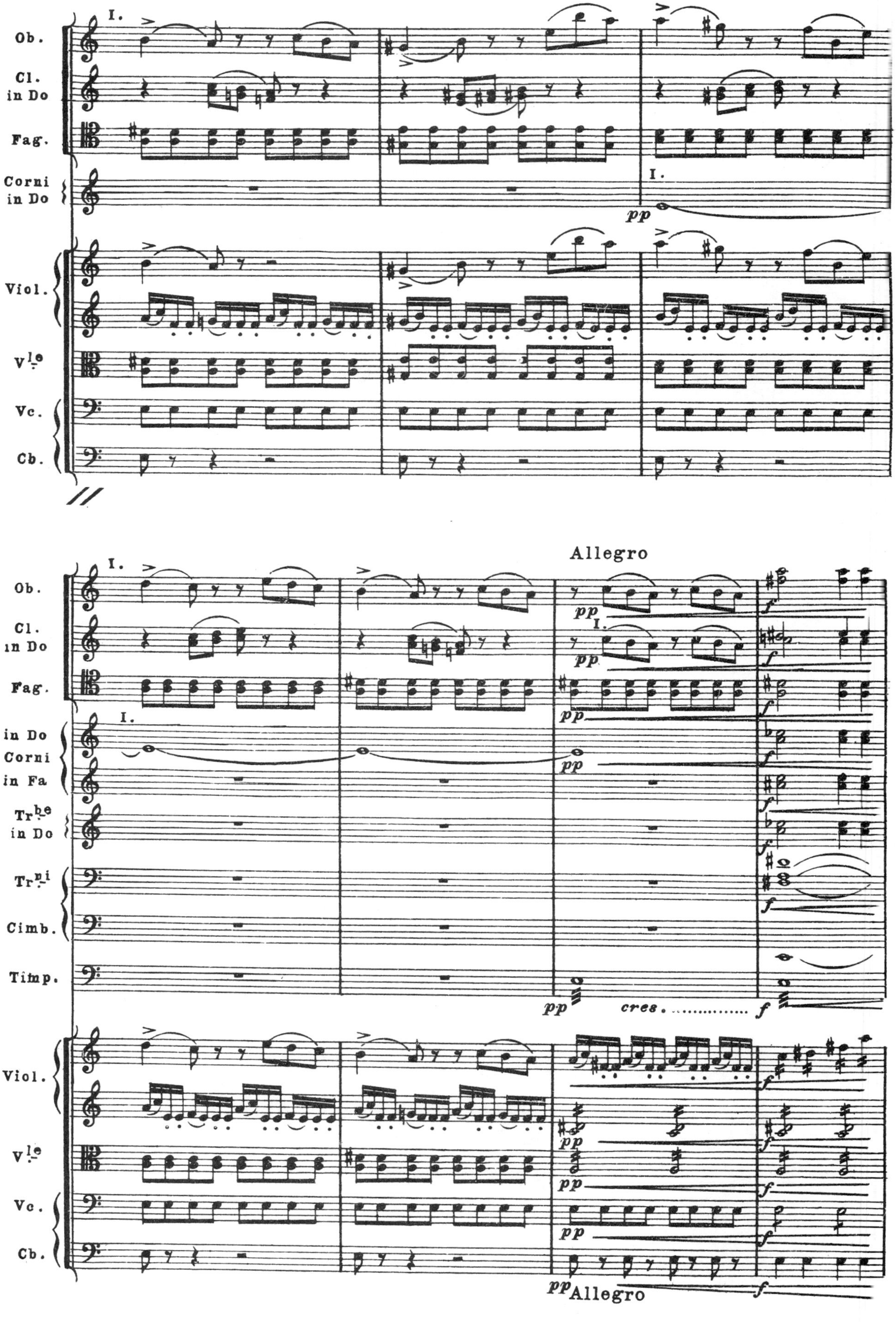
Ob.
Cl. in Do
Fag.
Corni in Do
Viol.
V. le
Vc.
Cb.
I.
pp
Allegro
in Do
Corni
in Fa
Tr. be in Do
Tr. ni
Cimb.
Timp.
cres. ....
f
pp Allegro

204

Duetto
(NORMA E ADALGISA)

SCENA VIII.

NORMA: Adalgisa! T'inoltra, o giovinetta, t'inoltra.

ADALGISA: (da lontano) Alma, costanza.

NORMA: *Recit.* E perchè tremi? Udii che grave a me segreto palesar tu voglia.

ADALGISA: È ver...

ADALGISA: Ma, deh! ti spoglia della celeste austerità che splende negli occhi tuoi... Dammi co-

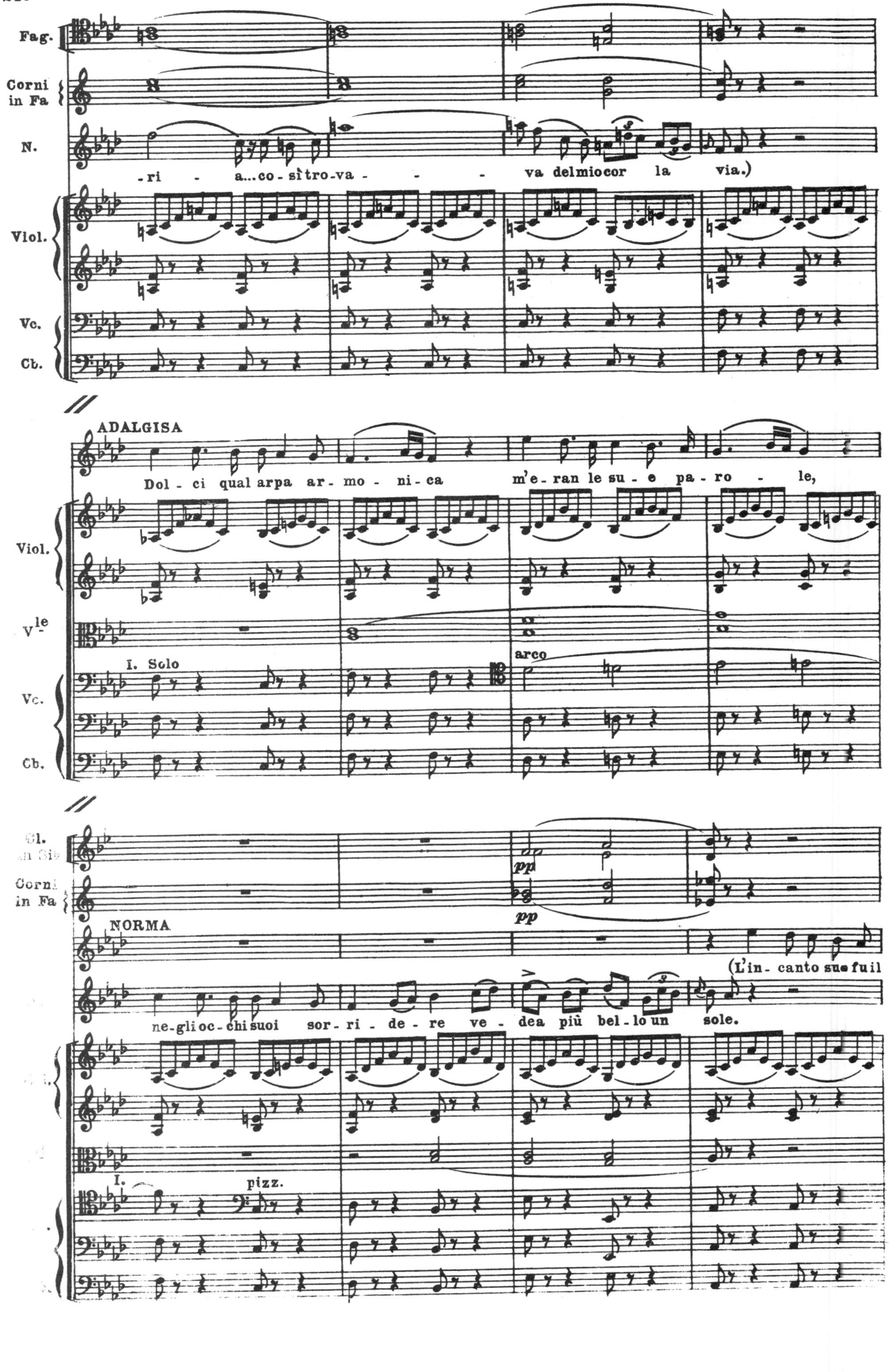
Fag.
Corni in Fa
N.
-ri - a...così tro-va - - - va del mio cor la via.)
Viol.
Vc.
Cb.
ADALGISA
Dol - ci qual arpa ar - mo - ni - ca m'e - ran le su - e pa - ro - le,
Viol.
Vle
I. Solo
arco
Vc.
Cb.
Cl. in Sib
Corni in Fa
pp
pp
NORMA
(L'in - canto sue fu il
ne-gli oc - chi suoi sor - ri - de - re ve - dea più bel - lo un sole.
I.
pizz.

218

219

226

Scena e Terzetto – Finale I.
(NORMA, ADALGISA E POLLIONE)

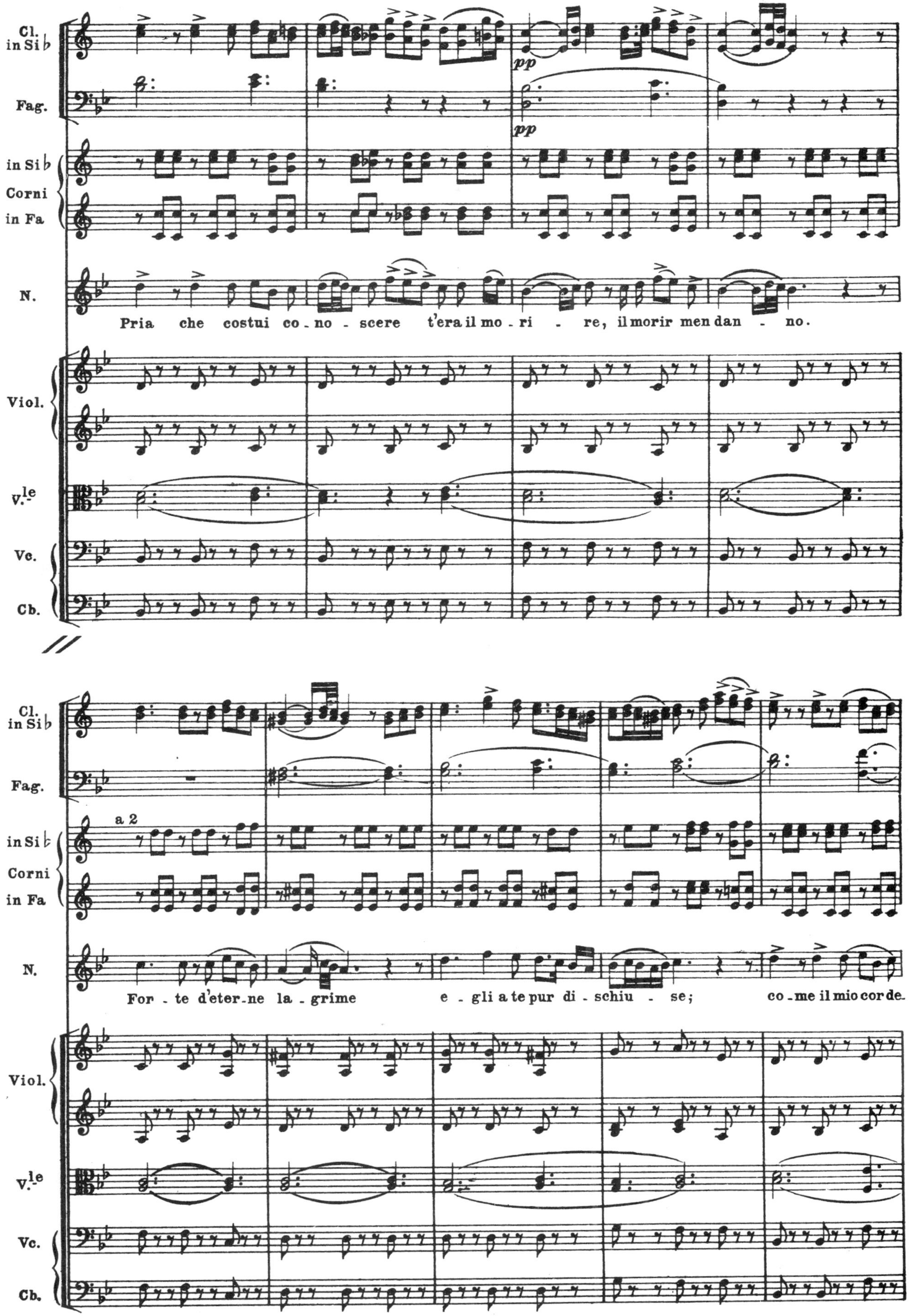
Cl. in Si♭
Fag.
pp
pp
in Si♭
Corni
in Fa
N.
Pria che costui co-no-scere t'era il mo-ri - re, il morir men dan - no.
Viol.
V.-le
Vc.
Cb.
Cl. in Si♭
Fag.
a 2
in Si♭
Corni
in Fa
N.
For - te d'eter-ne la - grime e - gli a te pur di - schiu - se; co-me il mio cor de-
Viol.
V.-le
Vc.
Cb.

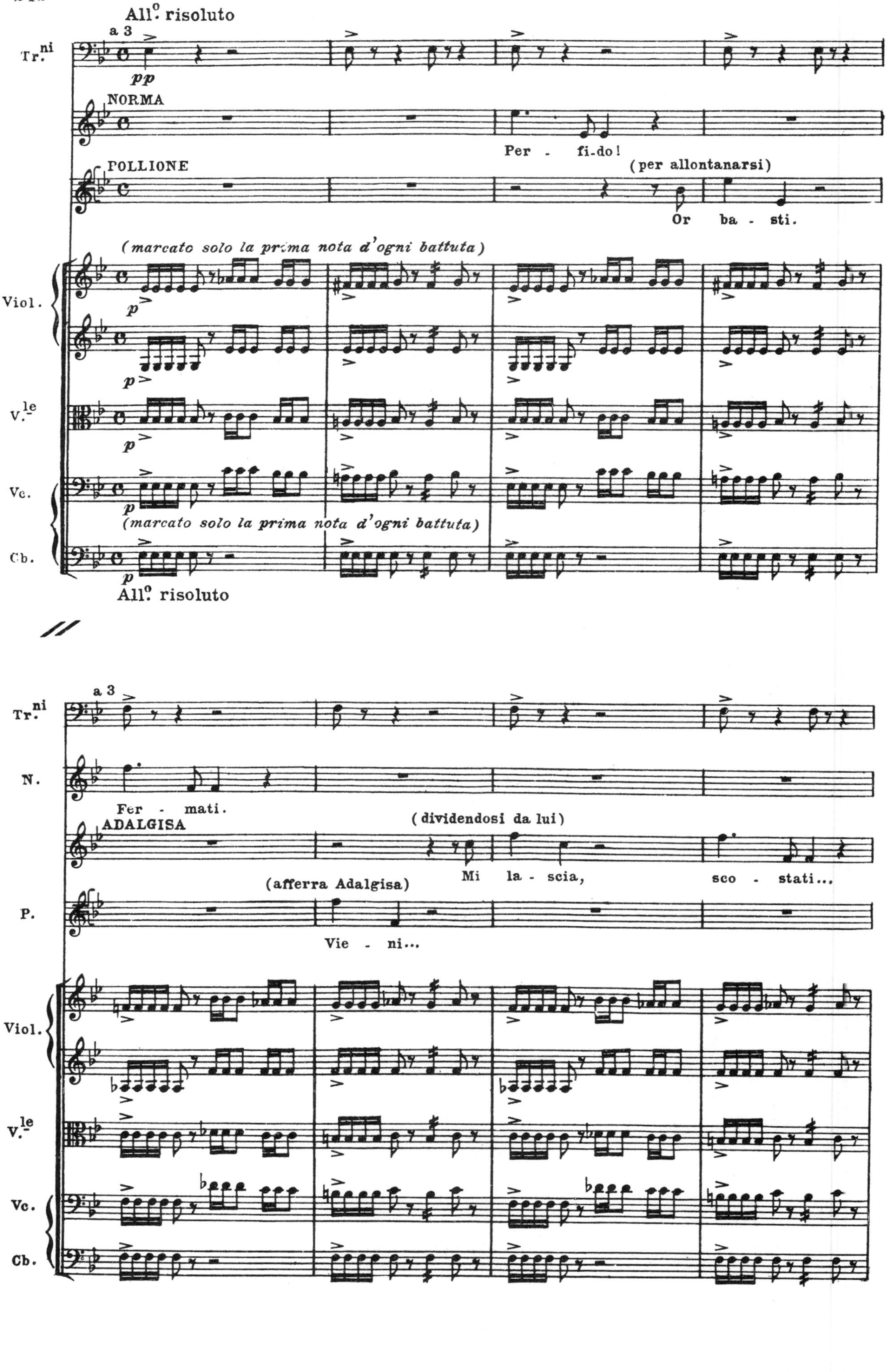
All.º risoluto
a 3
Tr.ni
pp
NORMA
Per - fi-do!
POLLIONE
(per allontanarsi)
Or ba - sti.
(marcato solo la prima nota d'ogni battuta)
Viol.
p
V.le
Vc.
(marcato solo la prima nota d'ogni battuta)
Cb.
All.º risoluto
a 3
Tr.ni
N.
Fer - mati.
ADALGISA
(dividendosi da lui)
Mi la - scia, sco - stati...
(afferra Adalgisa)
P.
Vie - ni...
Viol.
V.le
Vc.
Cb.

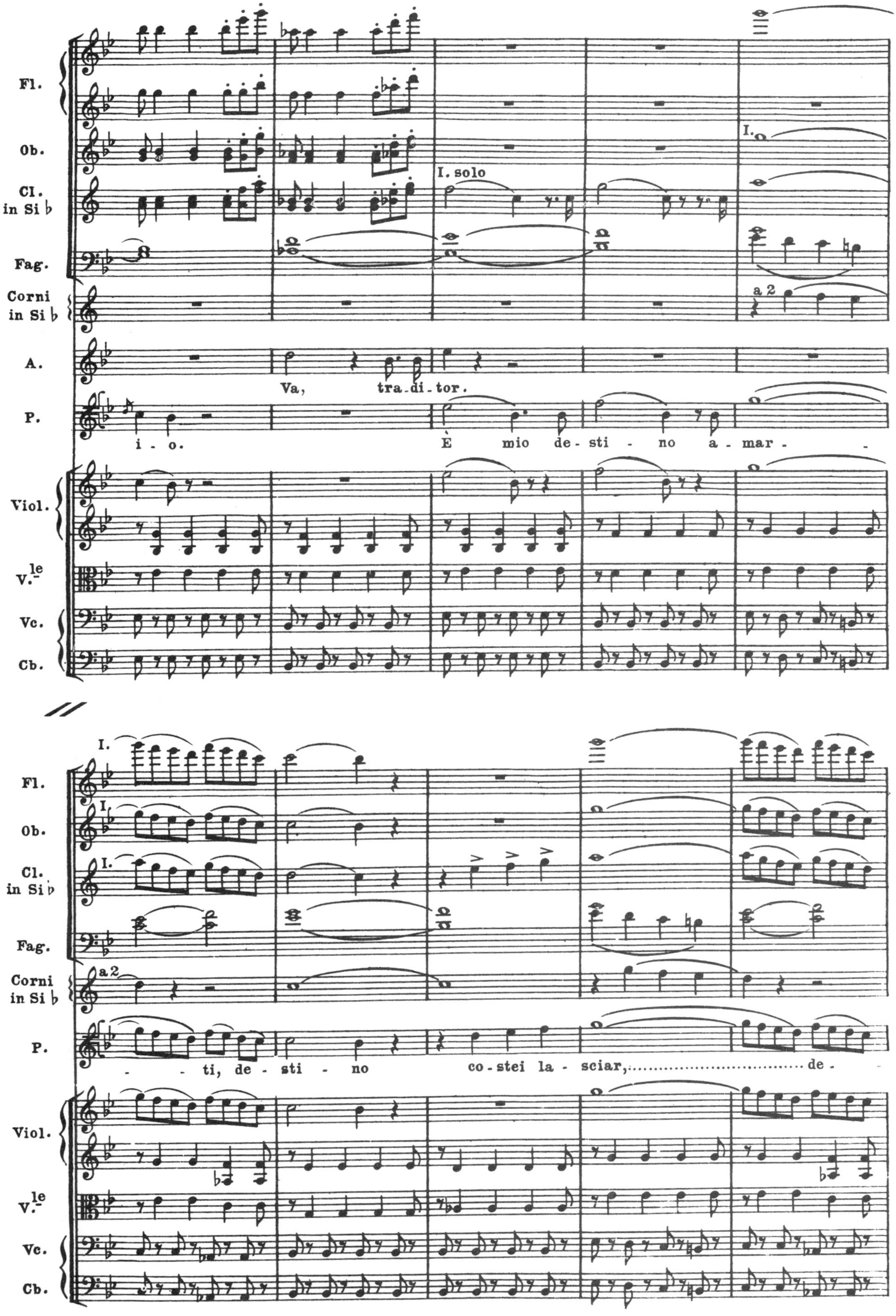
Fl.
Ob.
Cl. in Si ♭
Fag.
Corni in Si ♭
A.
P.
Viol.
V.le
Vc.
Cb.
I. solo
I.
a 2
Va, tra-di-tor.
i - o. È mio de-sti - no a-mar -
- - ti, de - sti - no co-stei la - sciar, de -

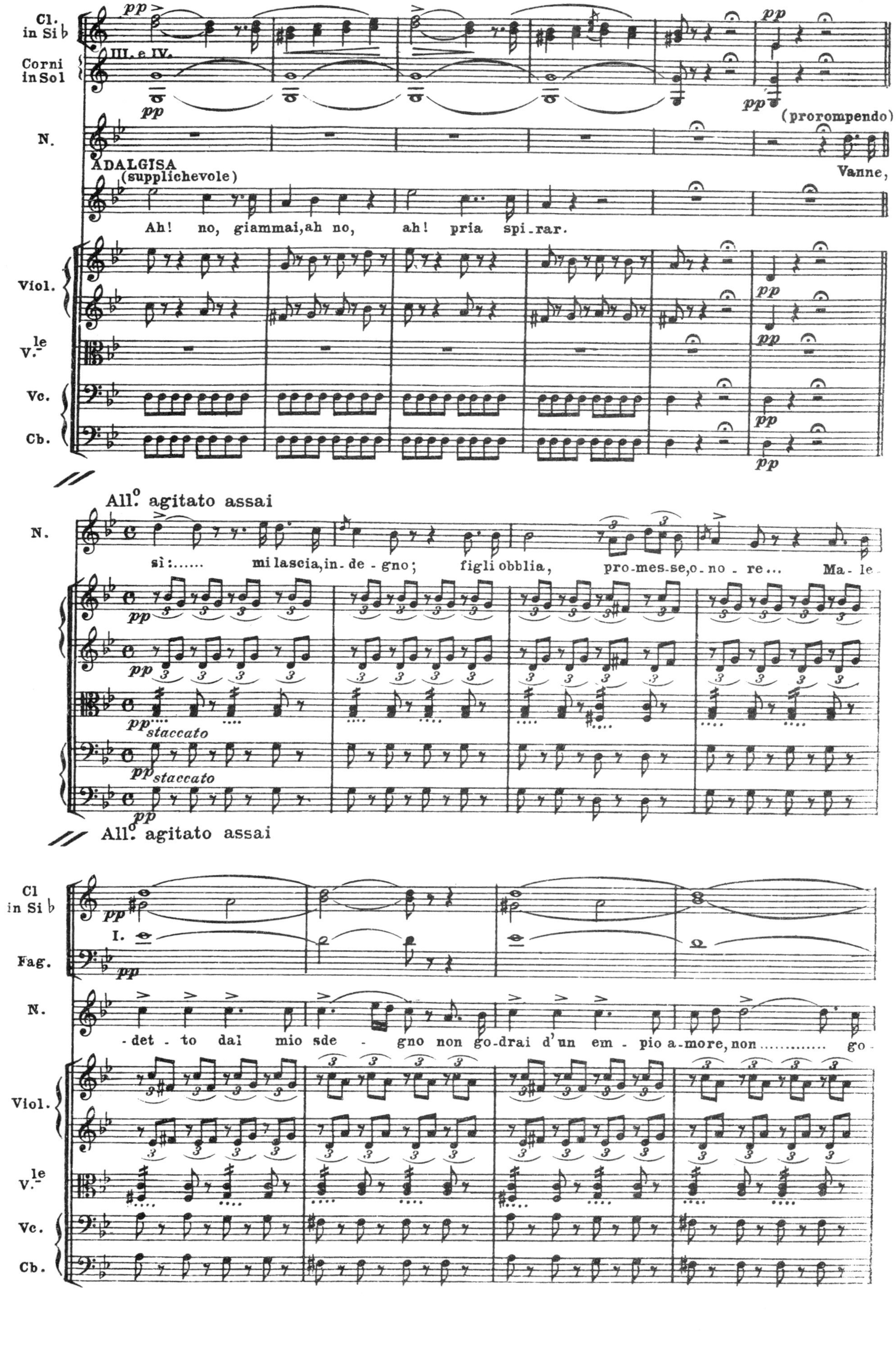
Cl. in Si♭
Corni in Sol
III. e IV.
N.
(prorompendo)
Vanne,
ADALGISA
(supplichevole)
Ah! no, giammai, ah no, ah! pria spi-rar.
Viol.
V.le
Vc.
Cb.
All.o agitato assai
sì:...... mi lascia, in-de-gno; figli obblia, pro-mes-se, o-no-re... Male-
staccato
All.o agitato assai
Fag.
-det-to dal mio sde-gno non go-drai d'un em-pio a-more, non............ go-

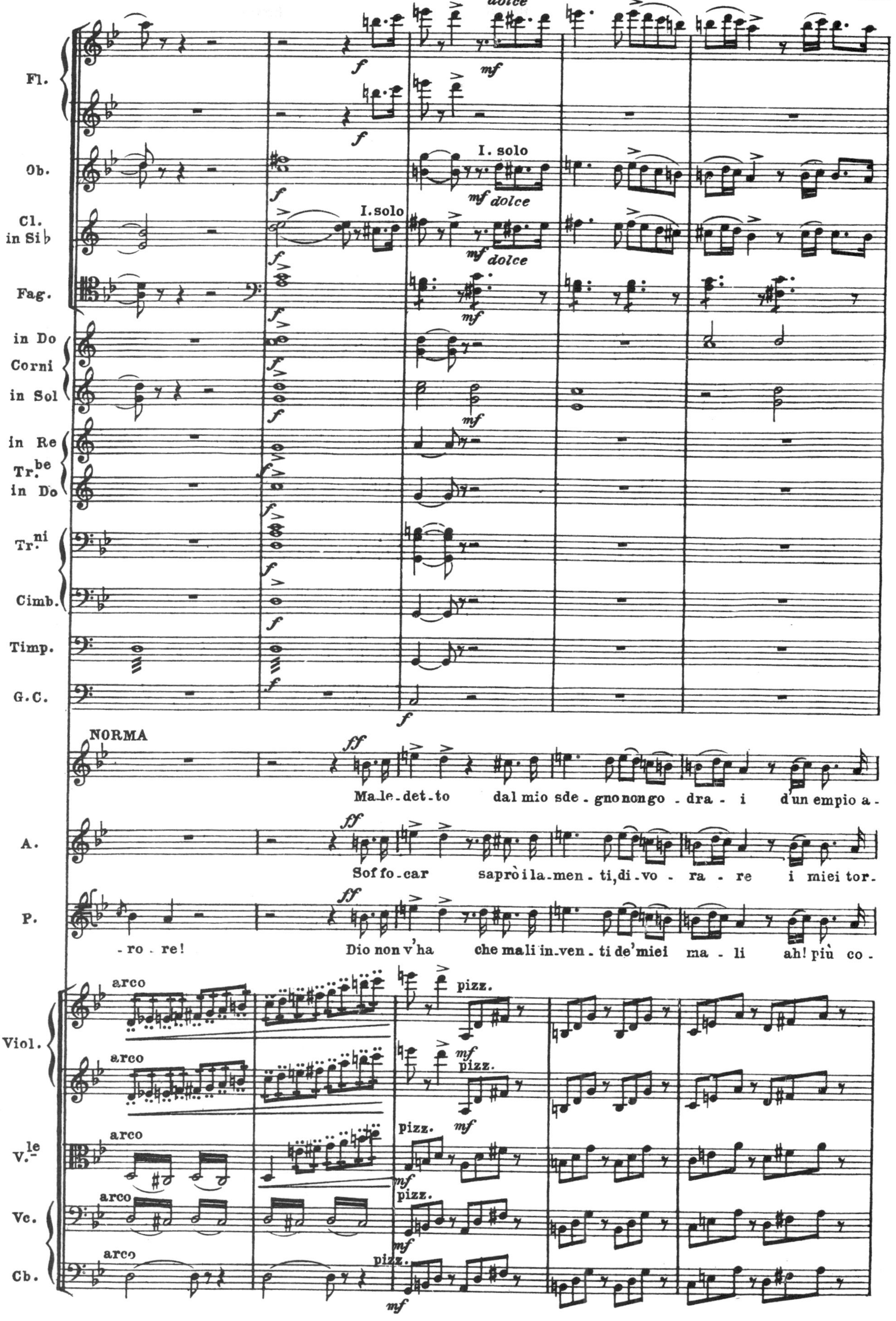
Fl.
dolce
mf
Ob.
I. solo
mf dolce
Cl. in Si♭
I. solo
mf dolce
Fag.
in Do
Corni
in Sol
in Re
Tr.be
in Do
Tr.ni
Cimb.
Timp.
G.C.
NORMA
ff
Ma_le_det_to dal mio sde_gno non go_dra_i d'un empio a_
A.
Sof fo_car saprò i la_men_ti, di_vo_ra_re i miei tor_
P.
_ro_re! Dio non v'ha che mali in_ven_ti de' miei ma_li ah! più co_
Viol.
arco
pizz.
V.le
Ve.
Cb.

254

256

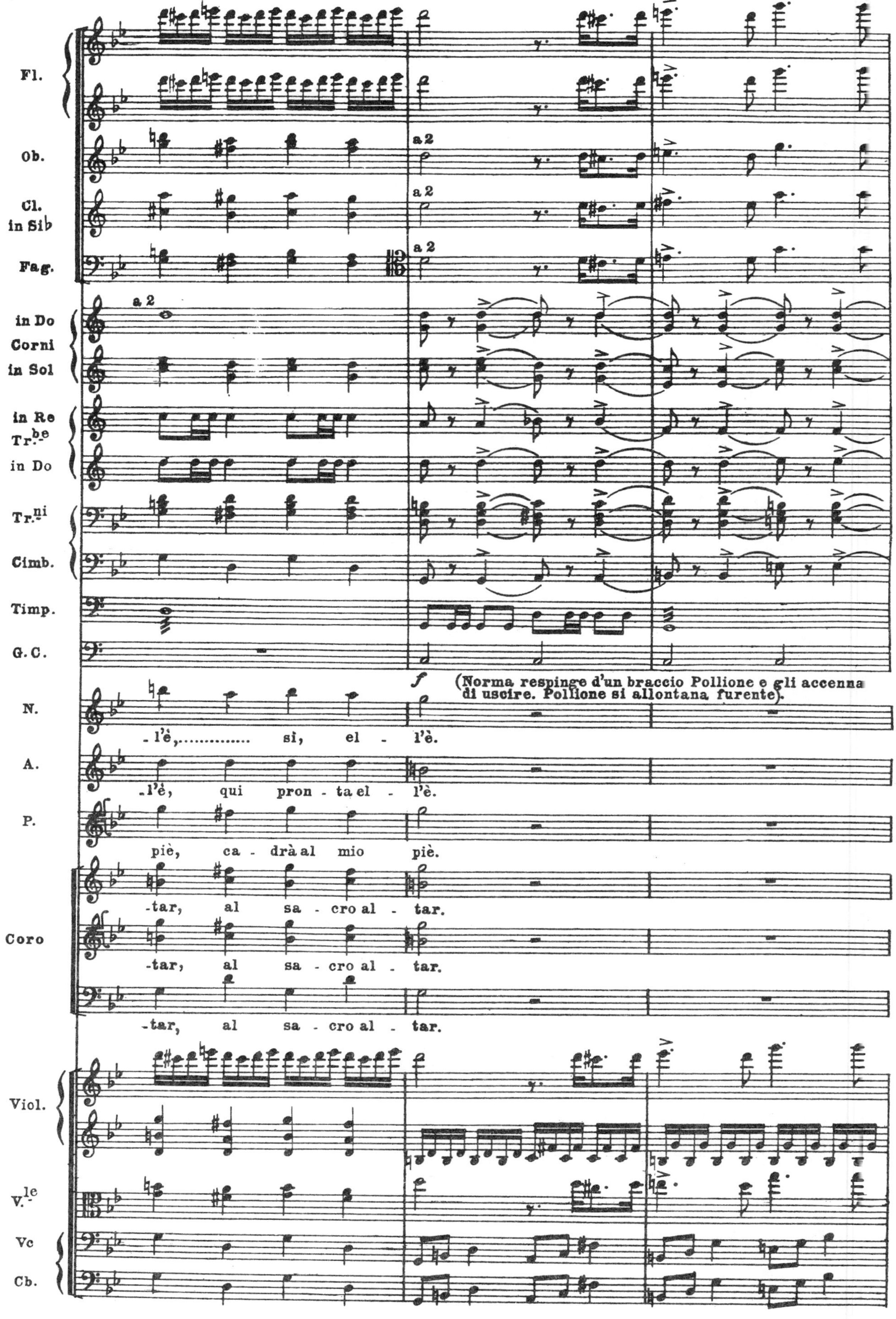
Fl.
Ob.
Cl. in Si♭
Fag.
a 2
in Do
Corni
in Sol
in Re
Tr.be
in Do
Tr.ni
Cimb.
Timp.
G.C.
(Norma respinge d'un braccio Pollione e gli accenna di uscire. Pollione si allontana furente).
N.
-l'è,............ si, el - l'è.
A.
-l'è, qui pron - ta el - l'è.
P.
piè, ca - drà al mio piè.
Coro
-tar, al sa - cro al - tar.
-tar, al sa - cro al - tar.
-tar, al sa - cro al - tar.
Viol.
V.le
Vc
Cb.

263

264

Fine dell'Atto Primo.

ATTO SECONDO
SCENA PRIMA.
Interno dell' abitazione di Norma.

Da una parte un letto romano coperto di pelle d'orso. I figli di Norma sono addormentati.

Introduzione

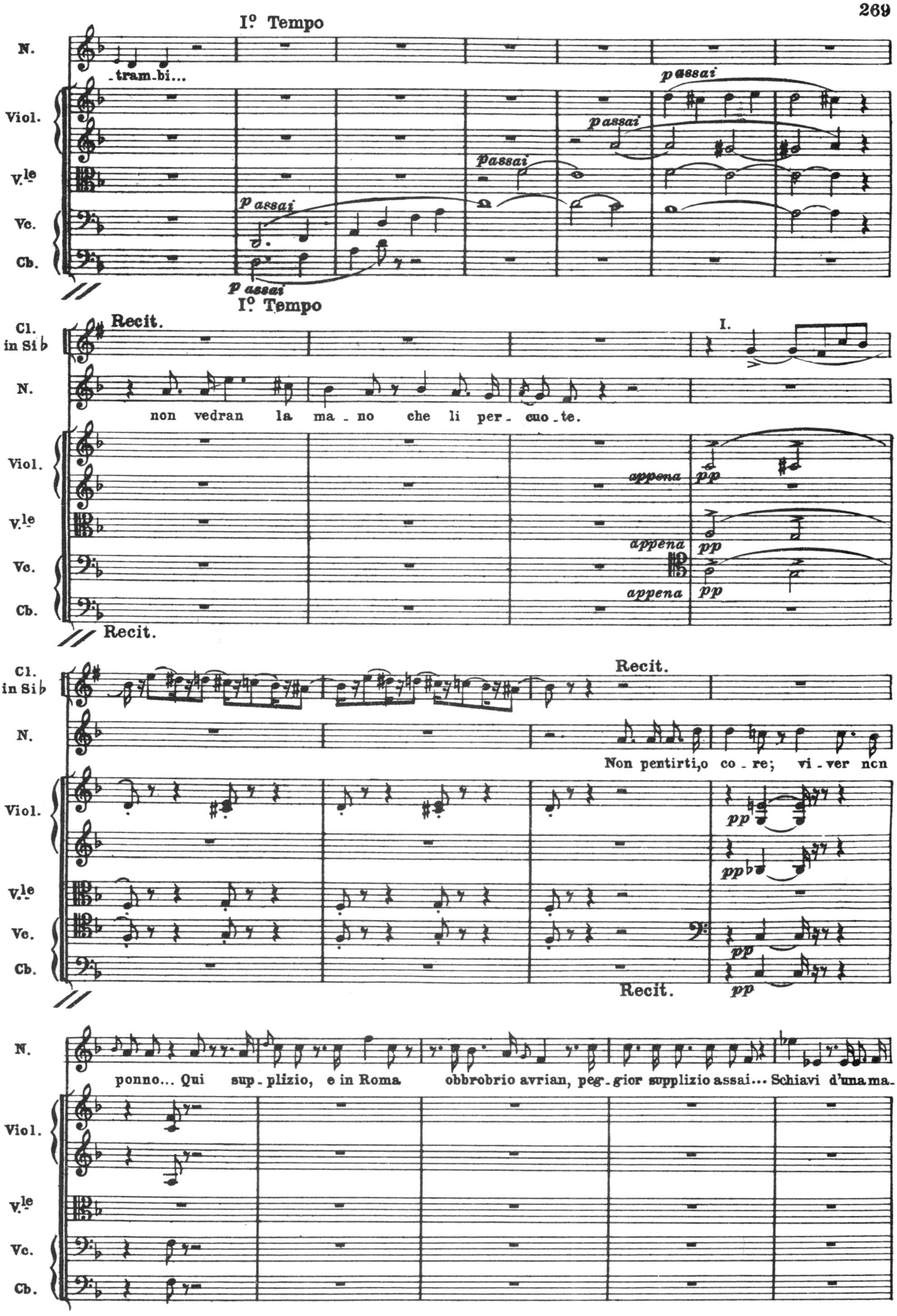
I° Tempo
N.
Viol.
V.le
Vc.
Cb.
_tram_bi...
p assai
Recit.
Cl. in Si♭
non vedran la ma_no che li per_cuo_te.
I.
appena pp
Non pentirti, o co_re; vi_ver non
ponno... Qui sup_plizio, e in Roma obbrobrio avrian, peg_gior supplizio assai... Schiavi d'una ma_

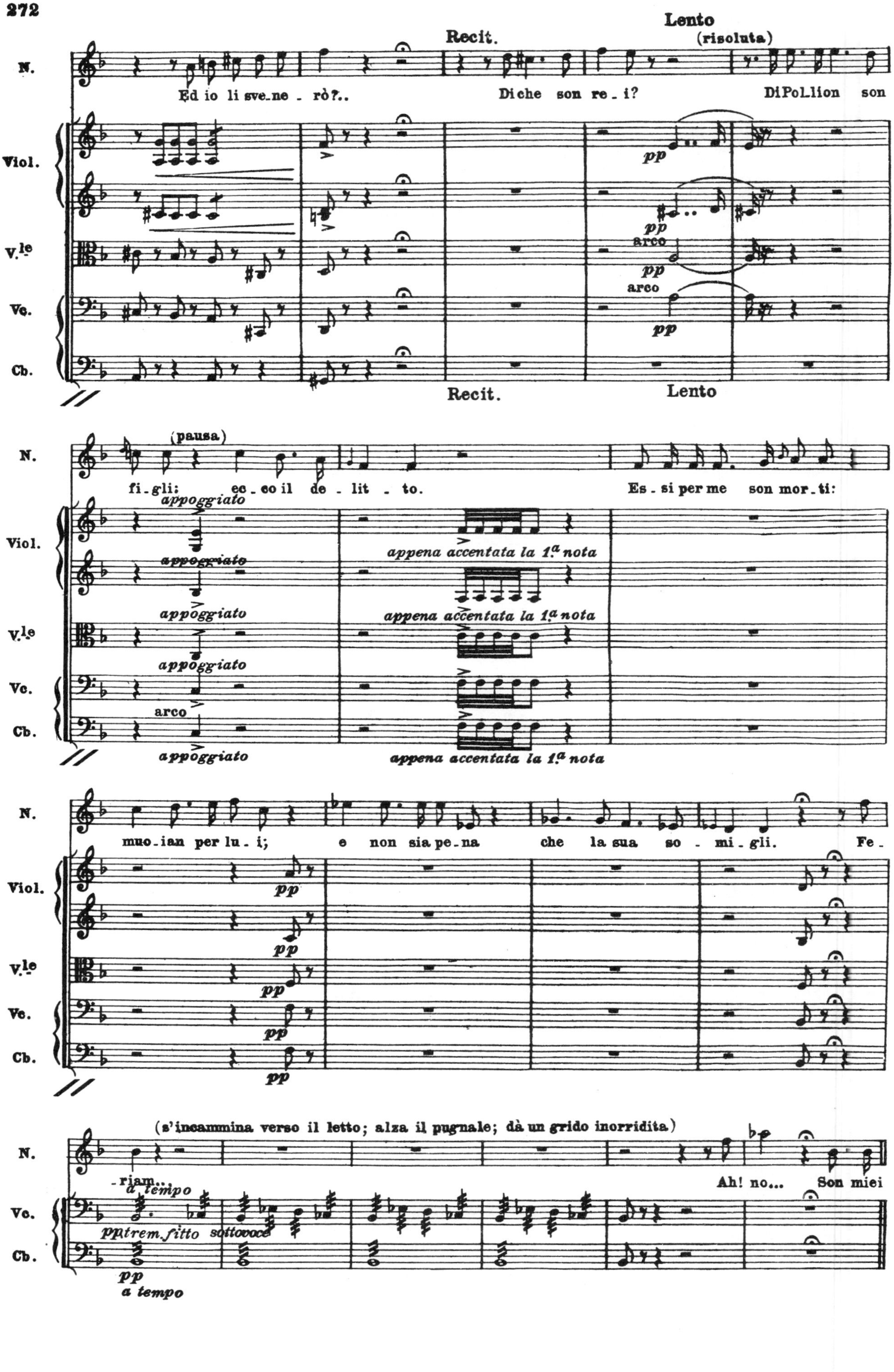
Lento
Recit.
(risoluta)
N.
Ed io li sve_ne _ rò?..
Diche son re _ i?
DiPol_lion son
Viol.
pp
V.le
arco
Vc.
Cb.
Recit.
Lento
(pausa)
fi_gli: ec_co il de _ lit _ to.
Es _ si per me son mor_ti:
appoggiato
appena accentata la 1.a nota
muo_ian per lu _ i; e non sia pe_na che la sua so _ mi_gli. Fe_
(s'incammina verso il letto; alza il pugnale; dà un grido inorridita)
_riam...
Ah! no... Son miei
a tempo
pp trem. fitto sottovoce
pp
a tempo

Scena e Duetto
(NORMA e ADALGISA)

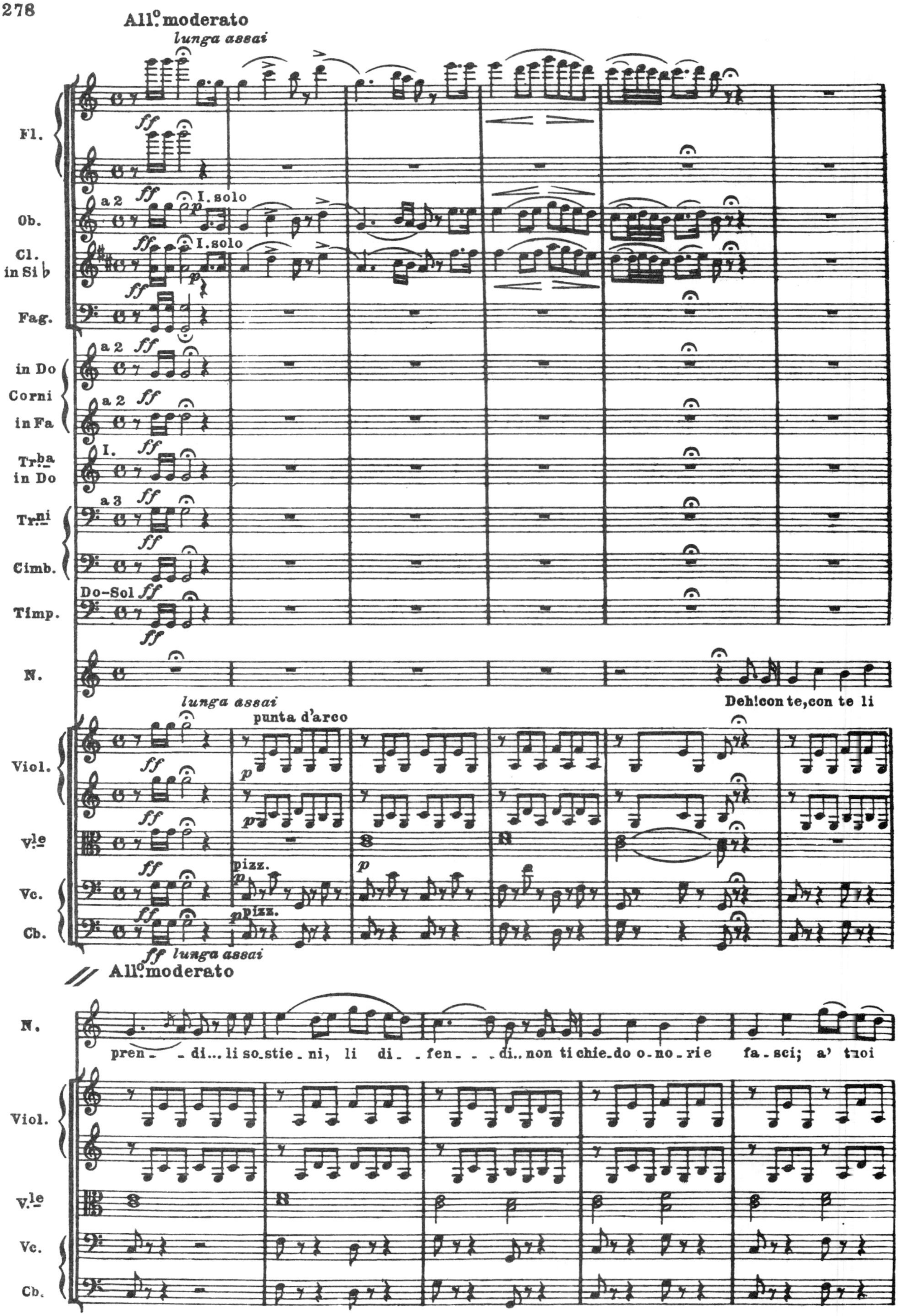
All° moderato
lunga assai
Fl.
Ob.
Cl. in Si♭
Fag.
in Do
Corni
in Fa
Tr.ba in Do
Tr.ni
Cimb.
Timp.
Do-Sol
a 2
a 3
I.
ff
I. solo
p
N.
Deh! con te, con te li
lunga assai
punta d'arco
Viol.
V.le
Vc.
Cb.
pizz.
lunga assai
All° moderato
N.
pren - di... li so-stie - ni, li di - fen - - di... non ti chie-do o-no-ri e fa-sci; a' tuoi
Viol.
V.le
Vc.
Cb.

280

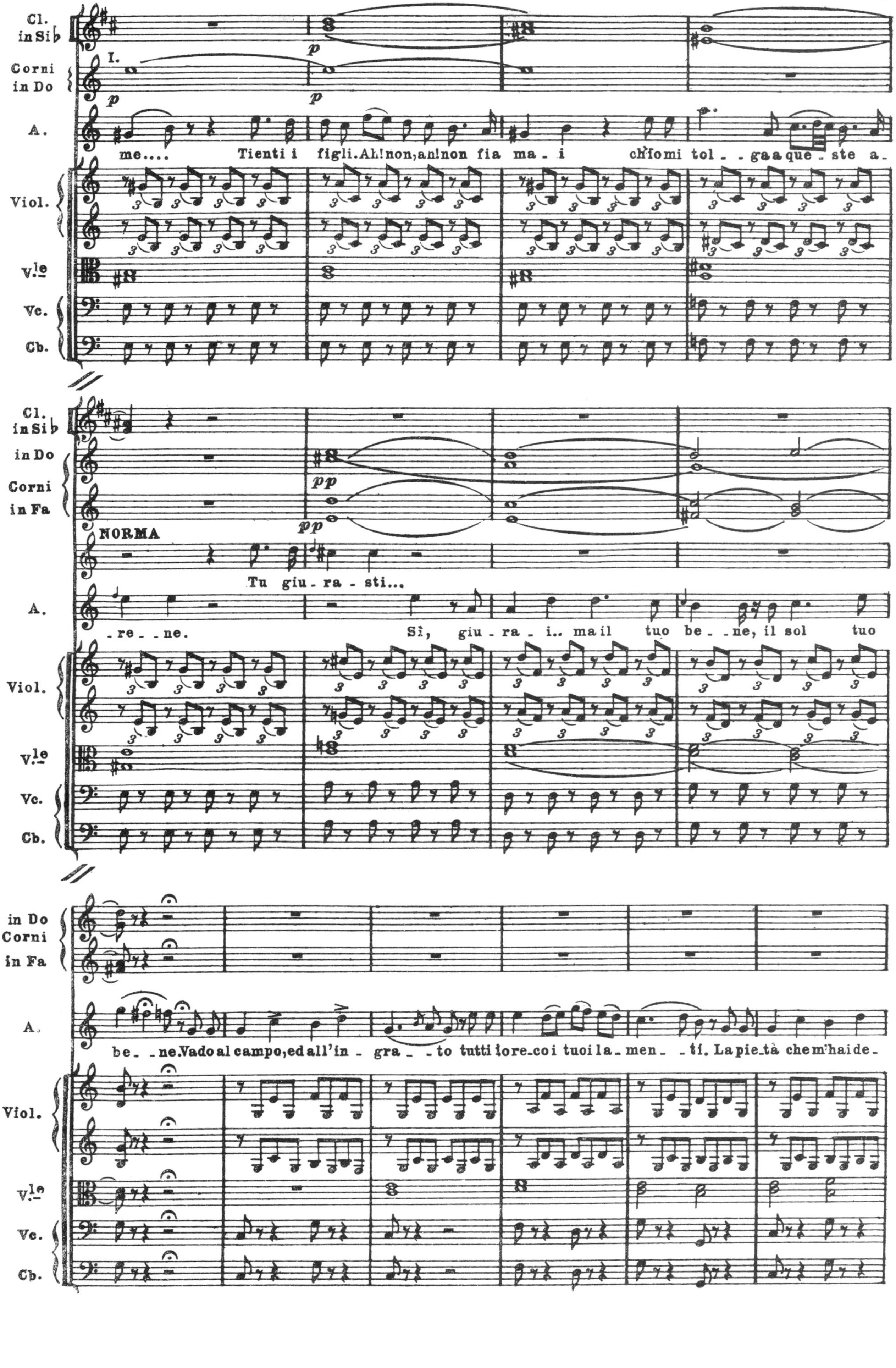
Cl. in Si♭
Corni in Do
I.
p
A.
me.... Tienti i figli. Ah! non, ah! non fia ma - i chi'omi tol - ga a que - ste a -
Viol.
V.le
Vc.
Cb.
Cl. in Si♭
in Do
Corni
in Fa
pp
NORMA
Tu giu - ra - sti...
- re - ne. Sì, giu - ra - i.. ma il tuo be - ne, il sol tuo
be - ne. Vado al campo, ed all'in - gra - to tutti i ore - coi tuoi la - men - ti. La pie - tà che m'hai de -

283

286

292

294

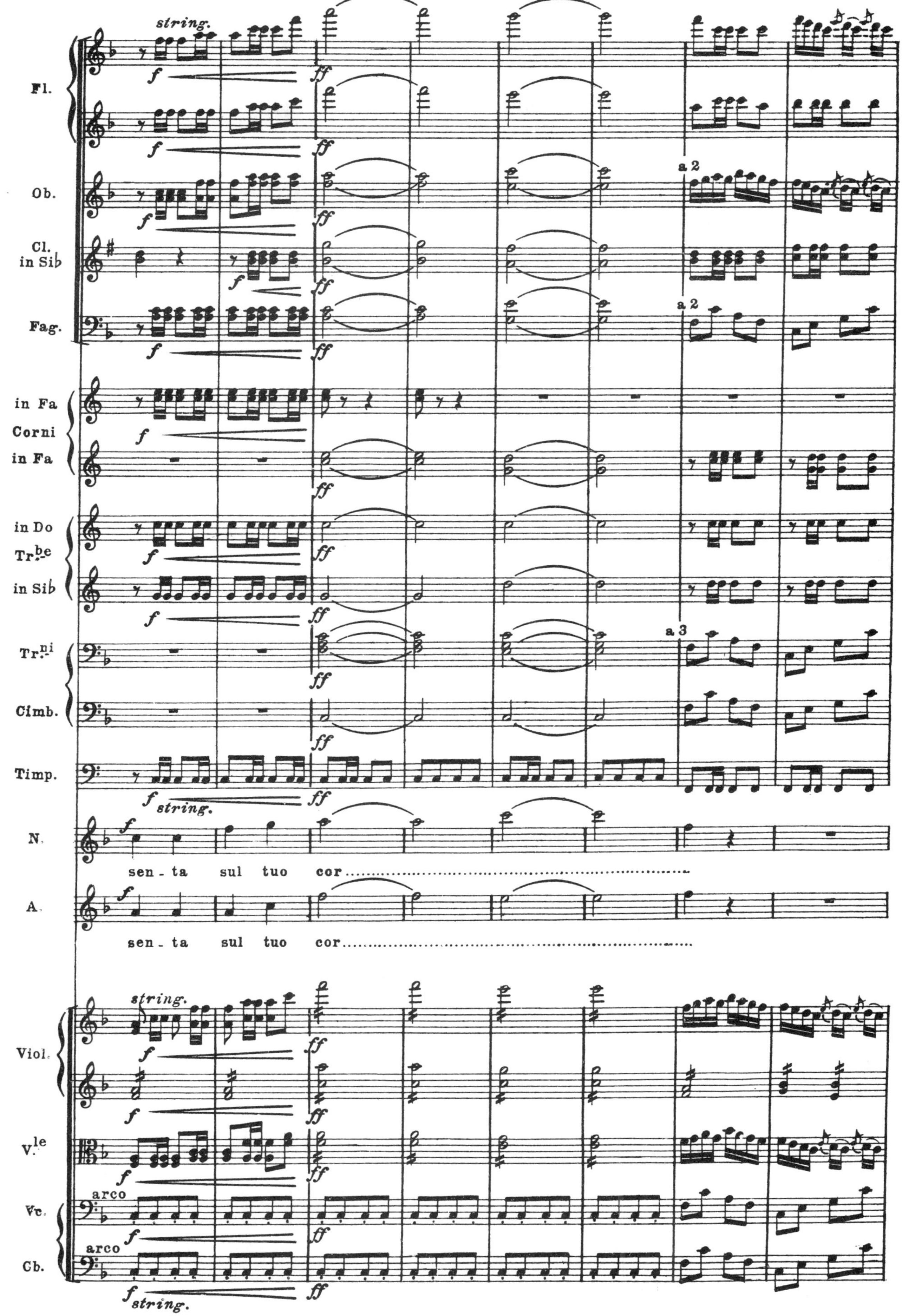
string.
Fl.
f
ff
Ob.
a 2
Cl. in Sib
Fag.
in Fa
Corni
in Fa
in Do
Tr.be
in Sib
Tr.ni
a 3
Cimb.
Timp.
string.
N.
sen - ta sul tuo cor
A.
sen - ta sul tuo cor
string.
Viol.
V.le
arco
Vc.
arco
Cb.
string.

300

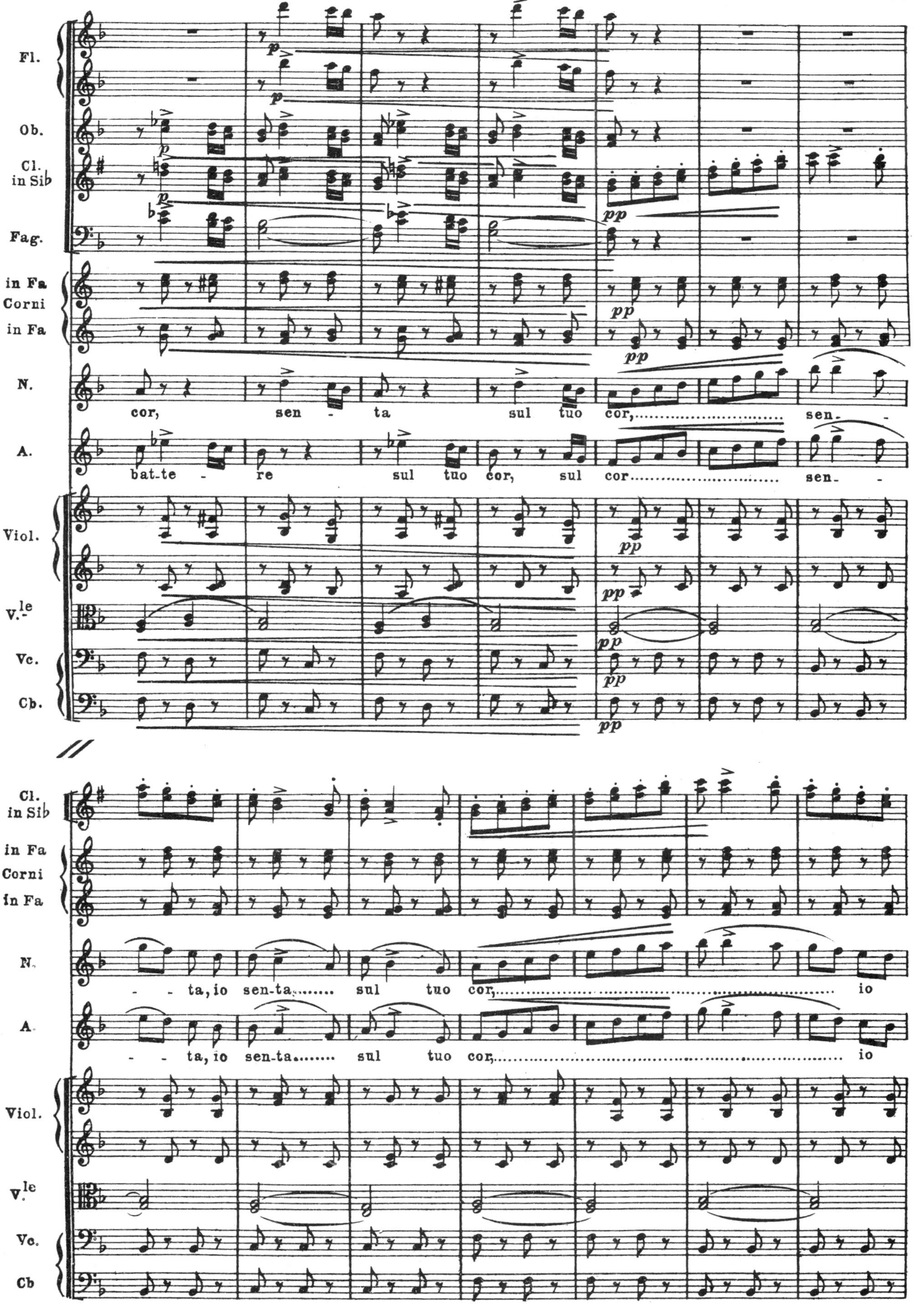
Fl.
Ob.
Cl. in Sib
Fag.
in Fa Corni in Fa
N.
cor, sen - ta sul tuo cor,.............................. sen-
A.
bat-te - re sul tuo cor, sul cor.............................. sen-
Viol.
V.le
Vc.
Cb.
Cl. in Sib
in Fa Corni in Fa
N.
- - ta, io sen-ta........ sul tuo cor,.............................. io
A.
- - ta, io sen-ta........ sul tuo cor,.............................. io
Viol.
V.le
Vc.
Cb

304

307

308

SCENA IV. Luogo solitario presso il bosco dei Druidi, cinto da burroni e da caverne. In fondo un lago attraversato da un ponte di pietra.

Coro e Sortita Oroveso

310

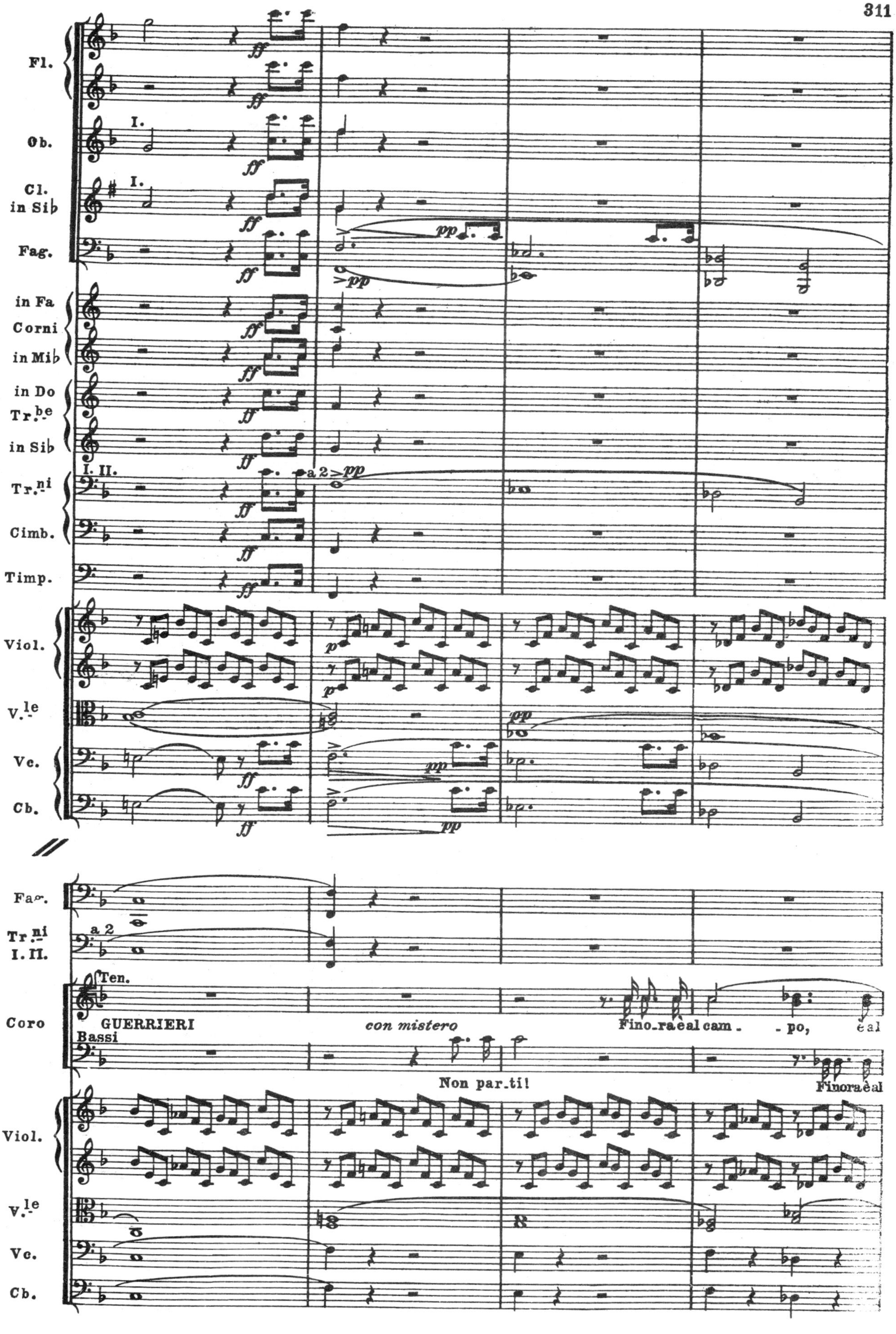
Fl.
Ob.
Cl. in Si♭
Fag.
Corni in Fa in Mi♭
Tr.be in Do in Si♭
Tr.ni
Cimb.
Timp.
Viol.
V.le
Vc.
Cb.
Coro
Ten.
Bassi
GUERRIERI
con mistero
Non par_ti!
Fino_ra è al cam_ - po, e al
Finora è al

314

315

316

318

320

324

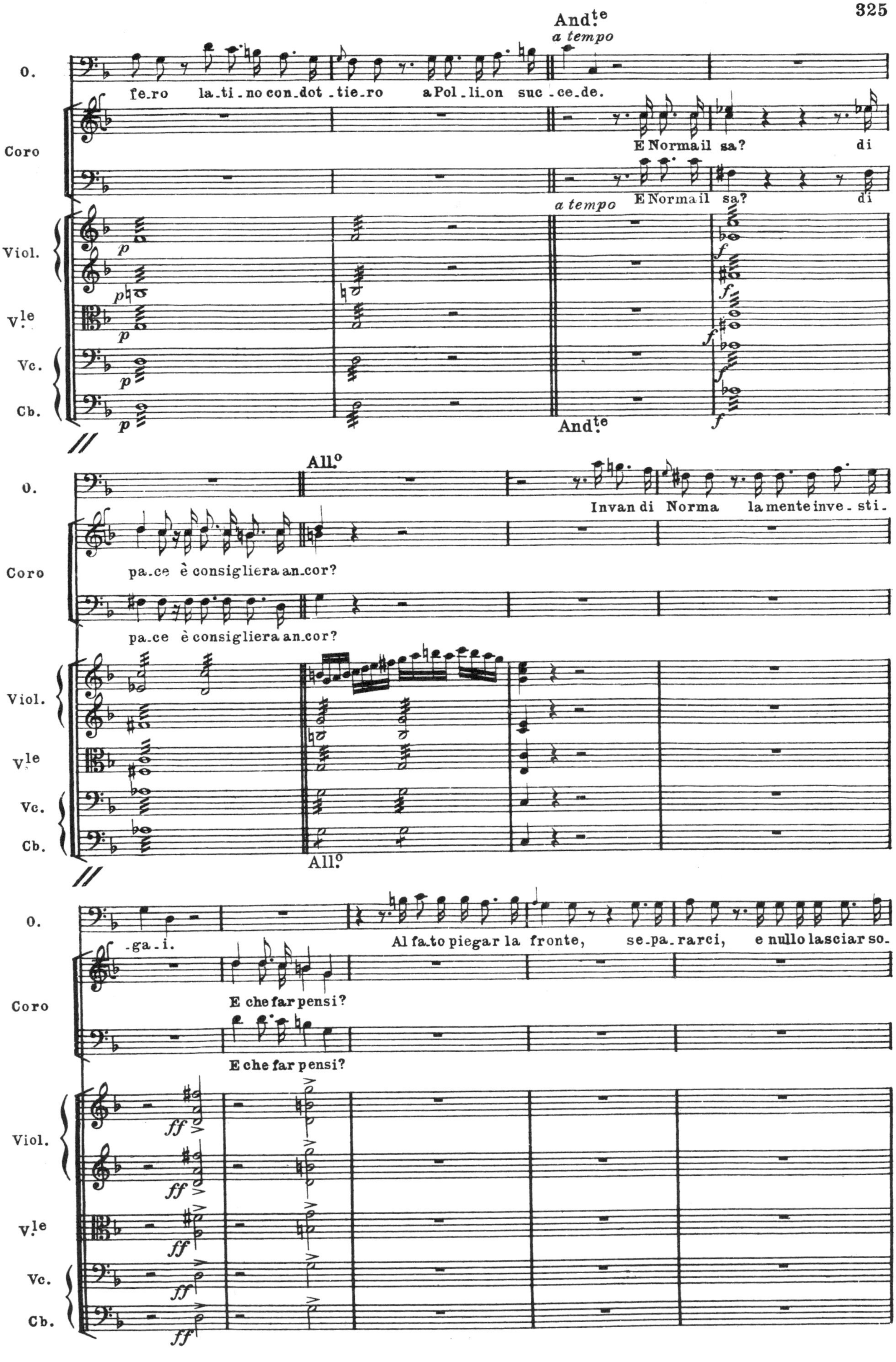
Andte
a tempo
O.
fe.ro la.ti.no con.dot.tie.ro a Pol.li.on suc.ce.de.
Coro
E Norma il sa? di
E Norma il sa? di
a tempo
Viol.
Vle
Vc.
Cb.
Andte
All°
Invan di Norma la mente inve.sti.
pa.ce è consigliera an.cor?
pa.ce è consigliera an.cor?
All°
.ga.i.
Al fa.to piegar la fronte, se.pa.rarci, e nullo lasciar so.
E che far pensi?
E che far pensi?

SCENA VI. Tempio d'Irminsul. Ara da un lato.

Recitativo e Coro

342

344 Scena VII.

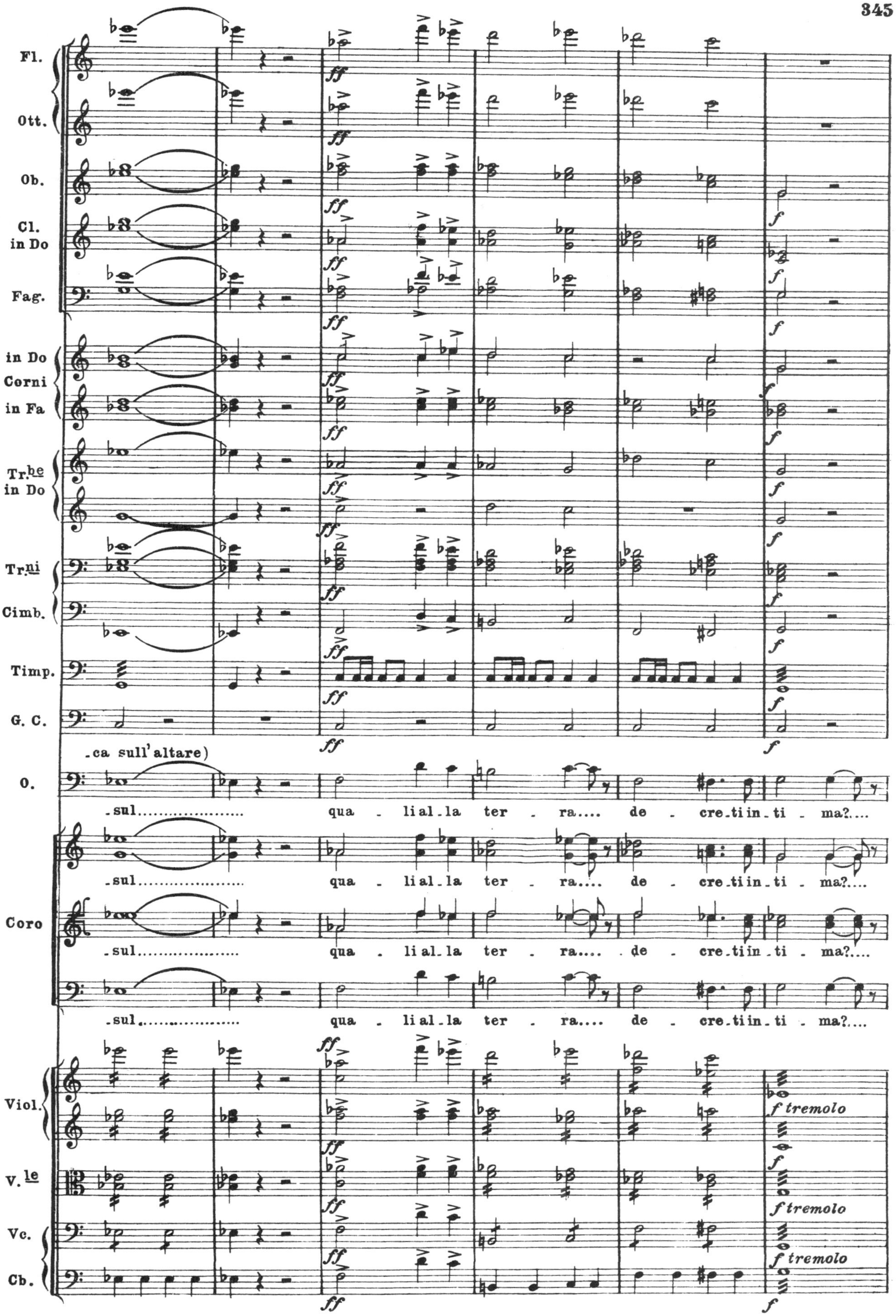
Fl.
Ott.
Ob.
Cl. in Do
Fag.
in Do
Corni
in Fa
Tr.be in Do
Tr.ni
Cimb.
Timp.
G. C.
.ca sull'altare)
O.
.sul...................... qua - li al.la ter - ra.... de - cre.ti in.ti - ma?....
.sul...................... qua - li al.la ter - ra.... de - cre.ti in.ti - ma?....
Coro
.sul...................... qua - li al.la ter - ra.... de - cre.ti in.ti - ma?....
.sul...................... qua - li al.la ter - ra.... de - cre.ti in.ti - ma?....
Viol.
V.le
Vc.
Cb.
ff
f
f tremolo

346

348

350

352

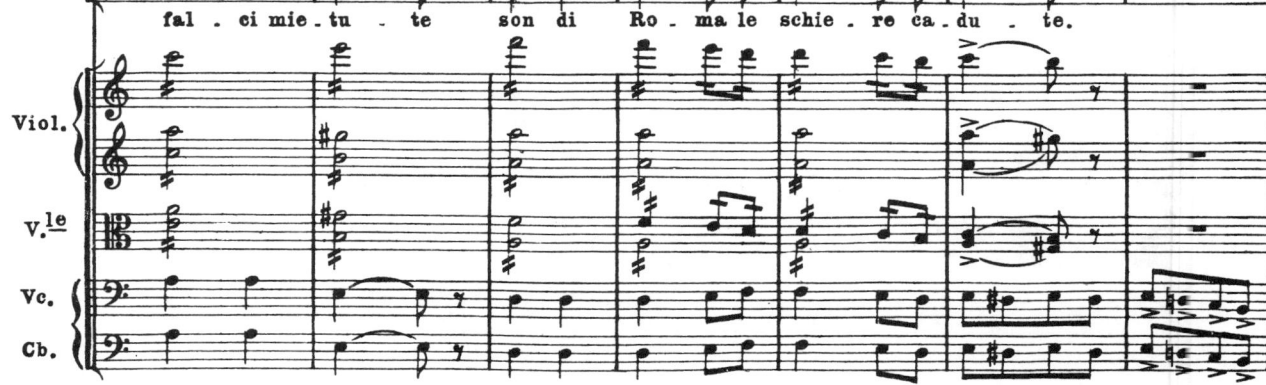

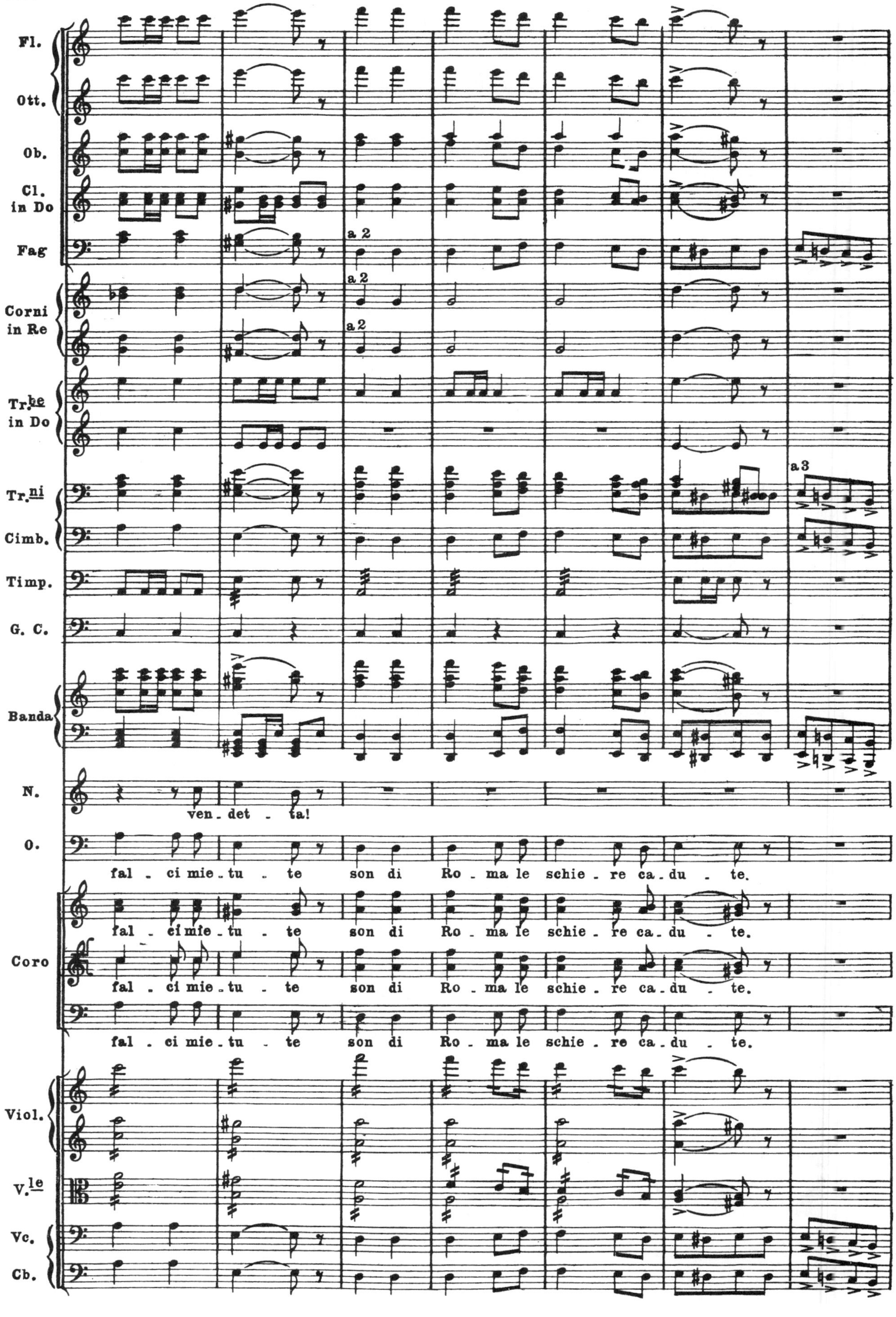
Fl.
Ott.
Ob.
Cl. in Do
Fag
a 2
Corni in Re
a 2
a 2
Tr.be in Do
Tr.ni
a 3
Cimb.
Timp.
G. C.
Banda
N.
ven - det - ta!
O.
fal - ci mie - tu - te son di Ro - ma le schie - re ca - du - te.
Coro
fal - ci mie - tu - te son di Ro - ma le schie - re ca - du - te.
fal - ci mie - tu - te son di Ro - ma le schie - re ca - du - te.
fal - ci mie - tu - te son di Ro - ma le schie - re ca - du - te.
Viol.
V.le
Vc.
Cb.

358

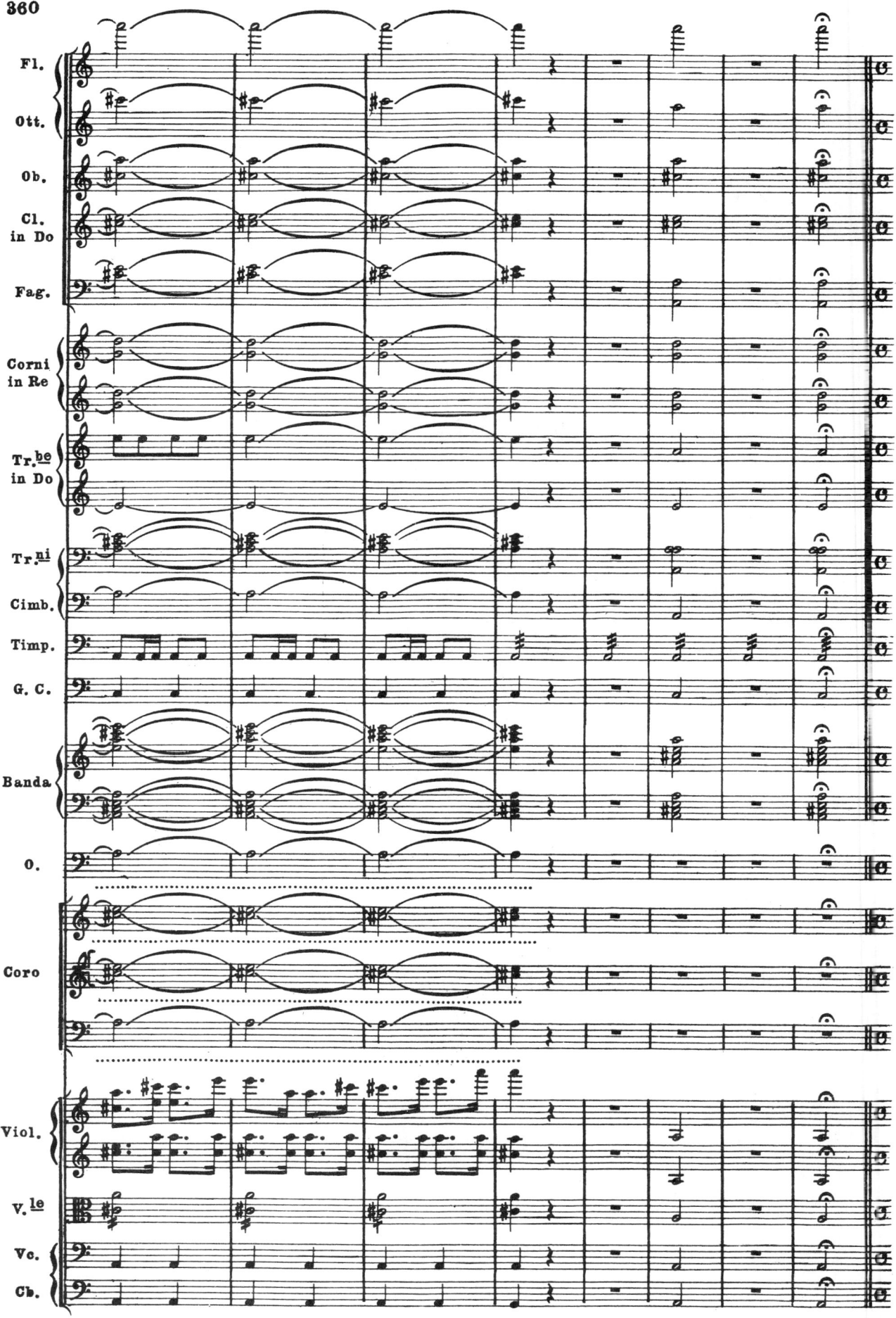

Scena e Duetto
(NORMA e POLLIONE)

362

371

SCENA X.

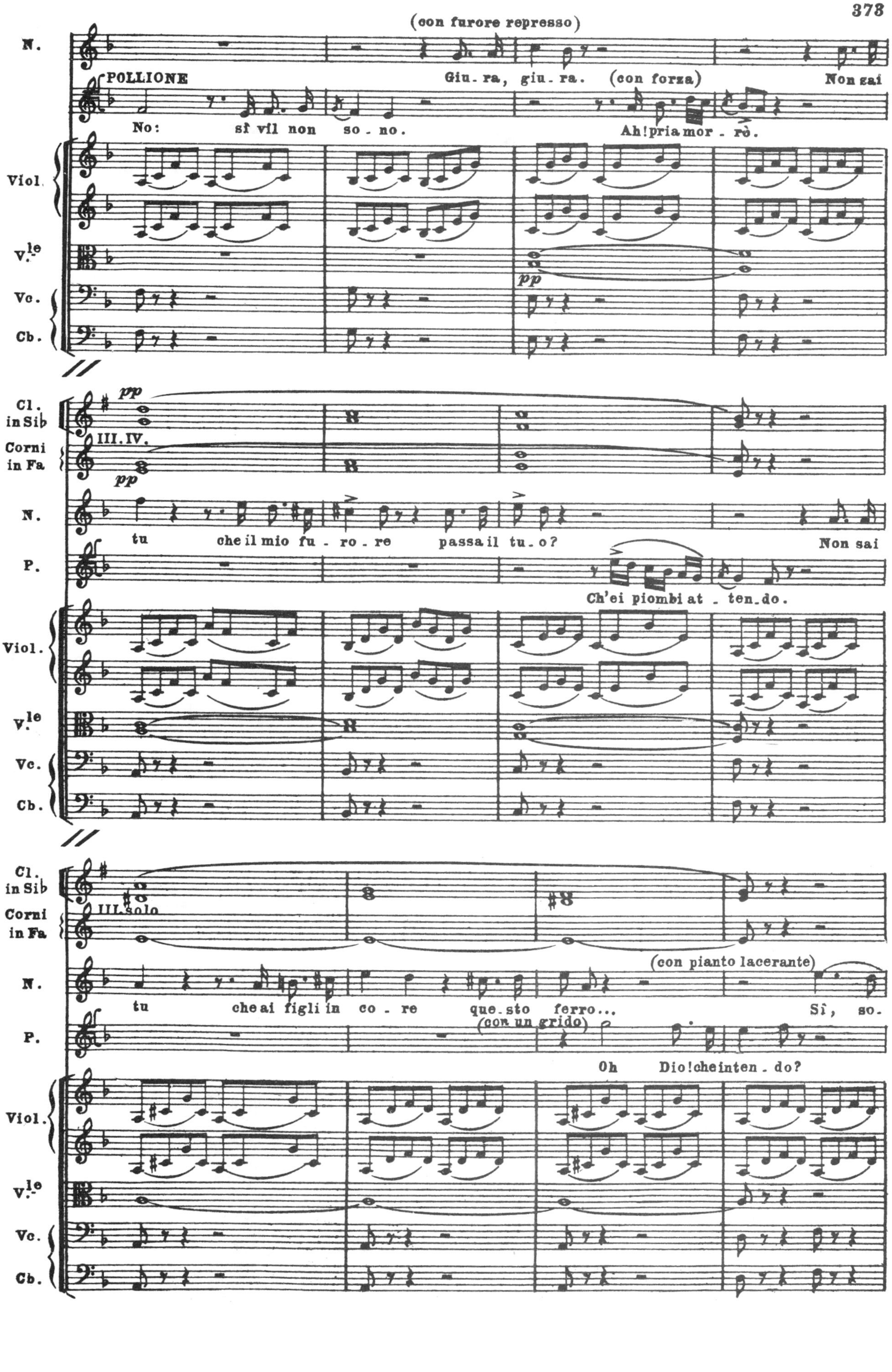
(con furore represso)
N.
POLLIONE
Giu_ra, giu_ra. (con forza) Non sai
No: sì vil non so_no. Ah! pria mor_rò.
Viol.
V.le
pp
Vc.
Cb.
Cl. in Sib
pp
Corni in Fa
III. IV.
pp
N.
tu che il mio fu_ro_re passa il tu_o? Non sai
P.
Ch'ei piombi at_ten_do.
Viol.
V.le
Vc.
Cb.
Cl. in Sib
Corni in Fa
III. solo
N.
tu che ai figli in co_re que_sto ferro...
(con pianto lacerante)
Sì, so.
P.
(con un grido)
Oh Dio! che inten_do?
Viol.
V.le
Vc.
Cb.

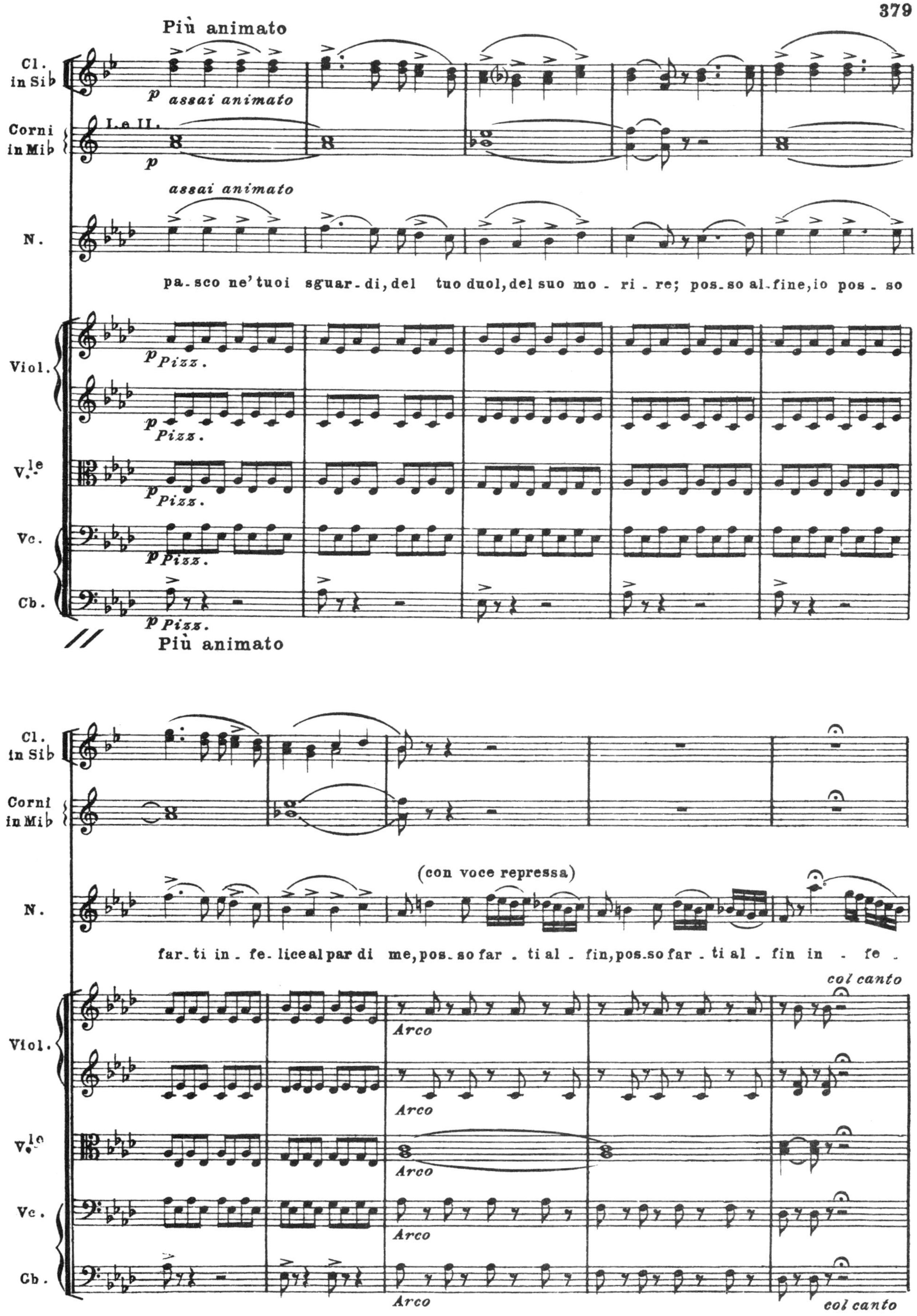
Più animato
Cl. in Sib
Corni in Mib
I. e II.
p
assai animato
N.
pa-sco ne'tuoi sguar-di, del tuo duol, del suo mo-ri-re; pos-so al-fine, io pos-so
Viol.
Pizz.
V.le
Vc.
Cb.
Più animato
(con voce repressa)
far-ti in-fe-lice al par di me, pos-so far-ti al-fin, pos-so far-ti al-fin in-fe-
col canto
Arco

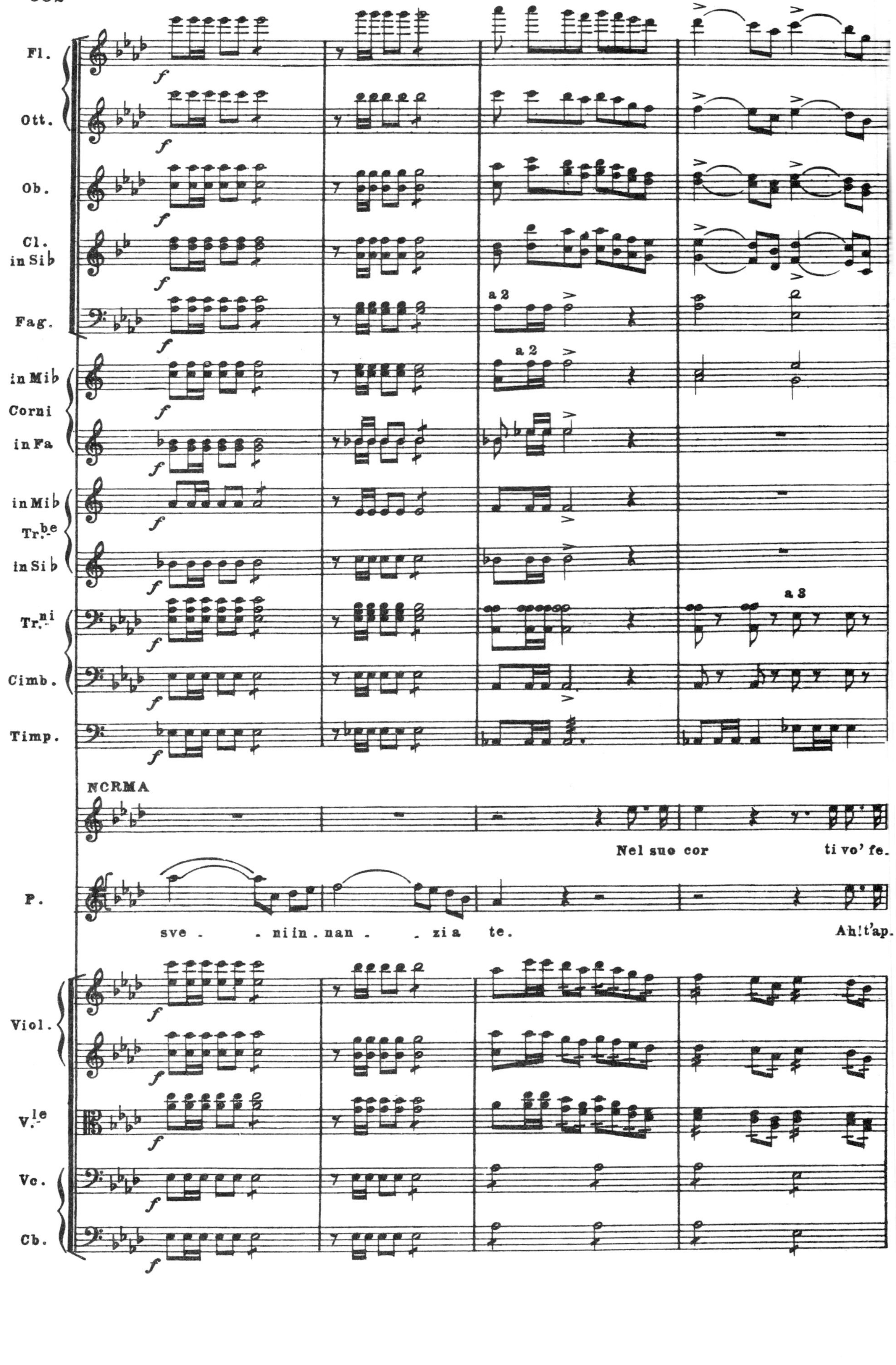
Fl.
Ott.
Ob.
Cl. in Sib
Fag.
a 2
in Mib
Corni
in Fa
in Mib
Tr.be
in Sib
Tr.ni
a 3
Cimb.
Timp.
NCRMA
Nel suo cor ti vo' fe.
P.
sve - - ni in - nan - - zi a te.
Ah! t'ap.
Viol.
V.le
Vc.
Cb.

386

390

Scena ultima ed Aria finale

406

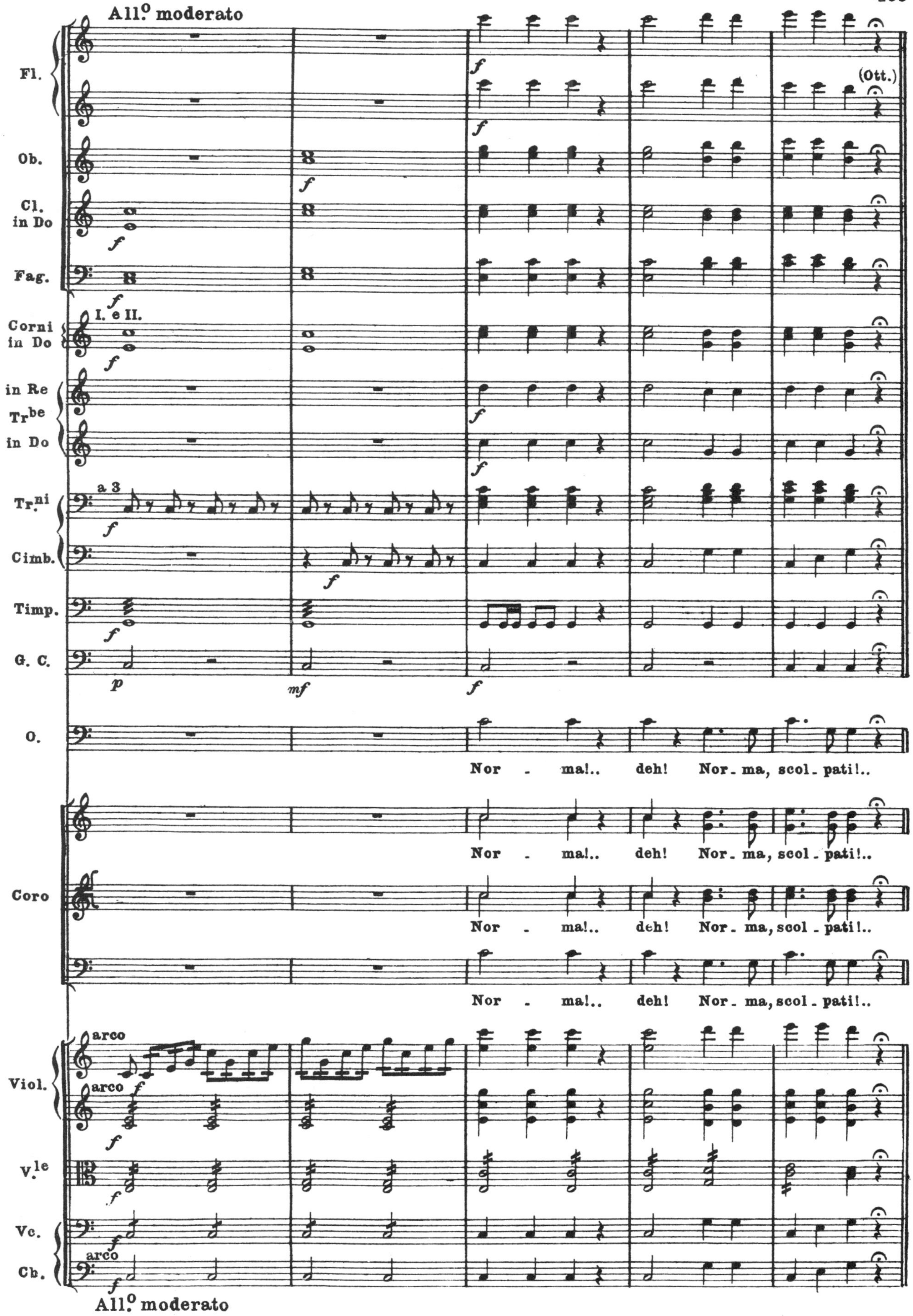
All.o moderato
Fl.
(Ott.)
Ob.
Cl. in Do
Fag.
Corni in Do
I. e II.
in Re
Trbe
in Do
a 3
Tr.ni
Cimb.
Timp.
G. C.
O.
Nor - ma!.. deh! Nor-ma, scol-pati!..
Coro
Nor - ma!.. deh! Nor-ma, scol-pati!..
Nor - ma!.. deh! Nor-ma, scol-pati!..
Nor - ma!.. deh! Nor-ma, scol-pati!..
arco
Viol.
arco
V.le
Ve.
arco
Cb.
All.o moderato

411

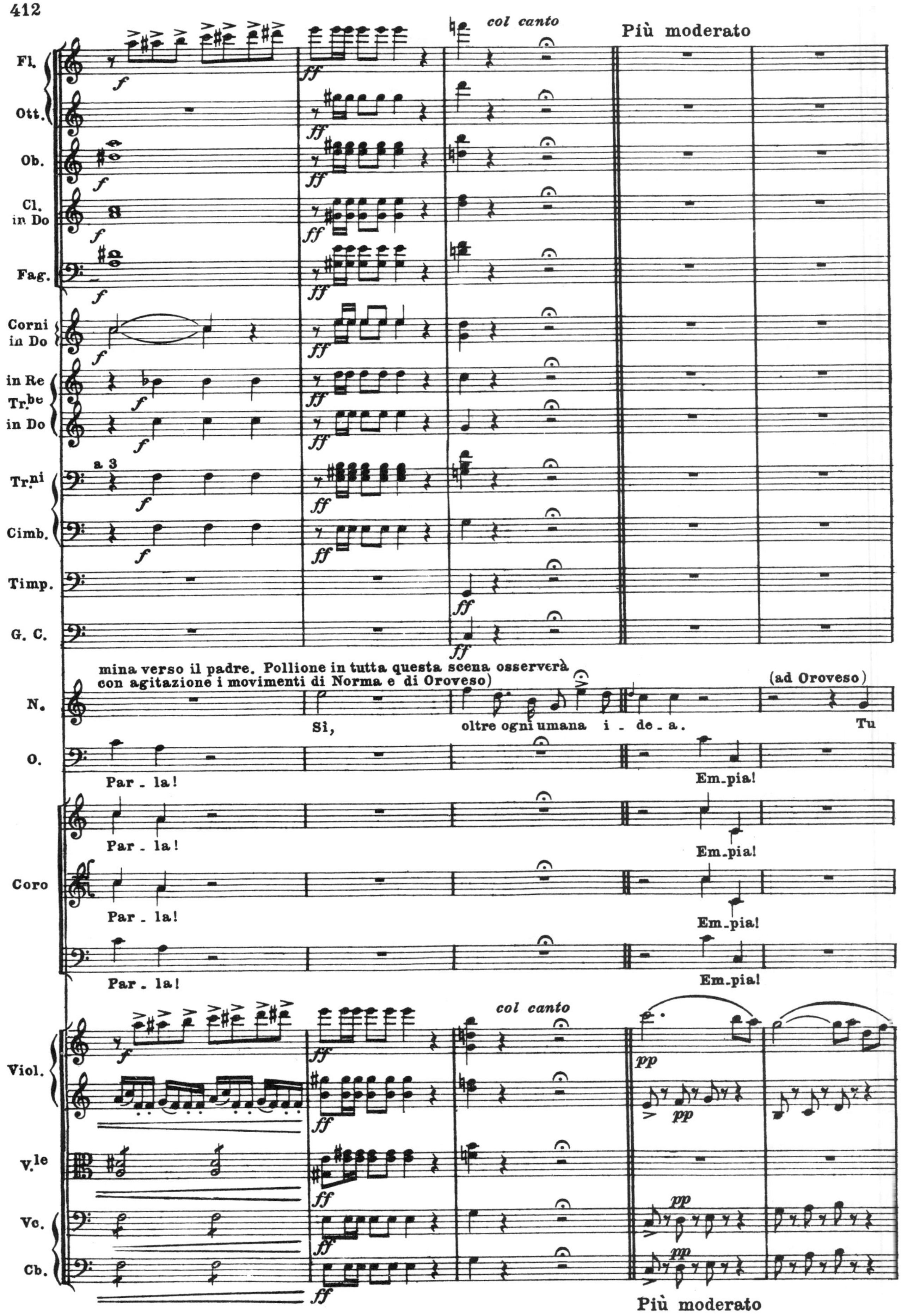

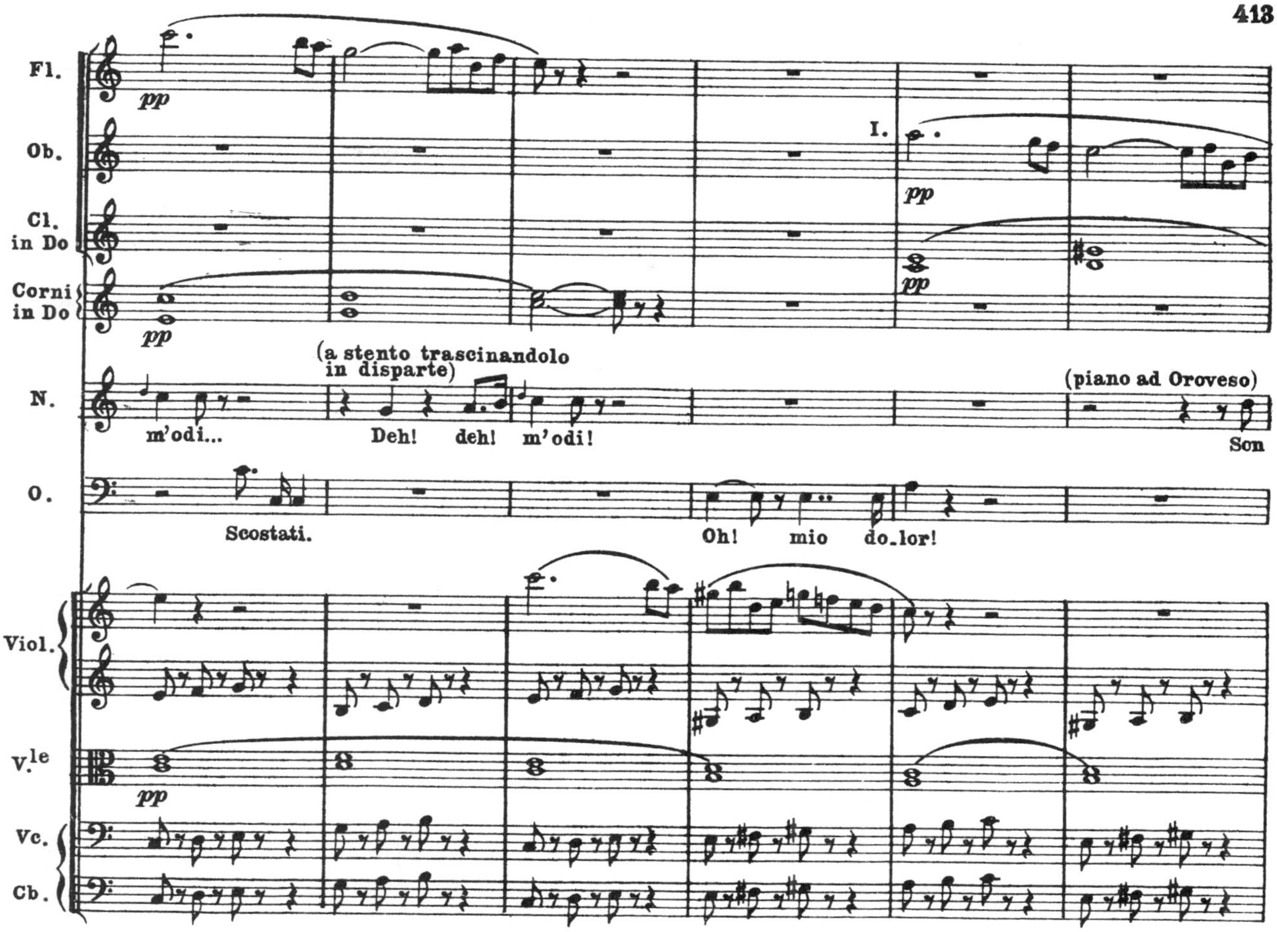
Fl.
Ob.
Cl. in Do
Corni in Do
N.
O.
Viol.
V.le
Vc.
Cb.
pp
I.
(a stento trascinandolo in disparte)
(piano ad Oroveso)
m'odi...
Deh! deh! m'odi!
Son
Scostati.
Oh! mio do_lor!

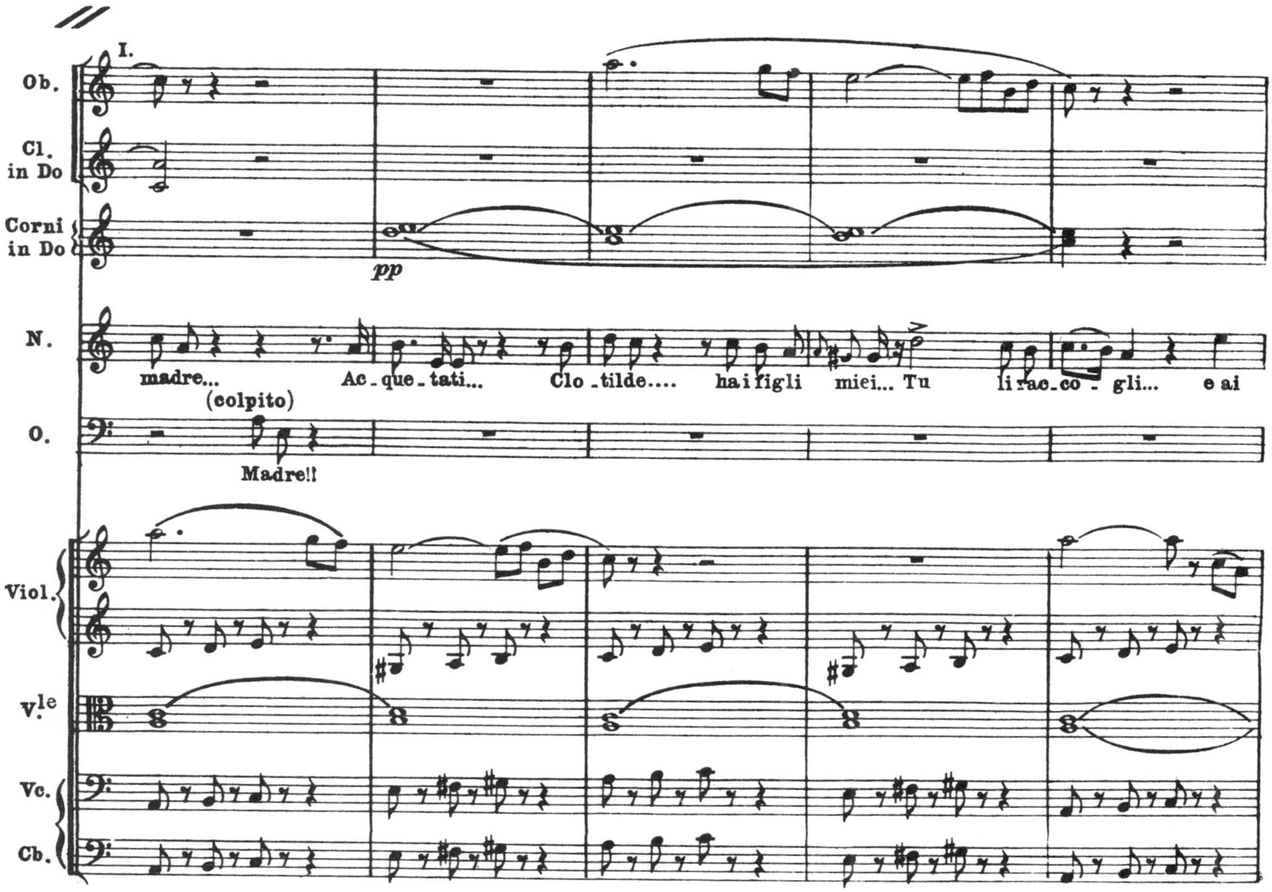
Ob.
Cl. in Do
Corni in Do
N.
O.
Viol.
V.le
Vc.
Cb.
I.
pp
madre...
Ac_que_tati...
Clo_tilde....
hai figli
miei... Tu
li rac_co_gli...
e ai
(colpito)
Madre!!

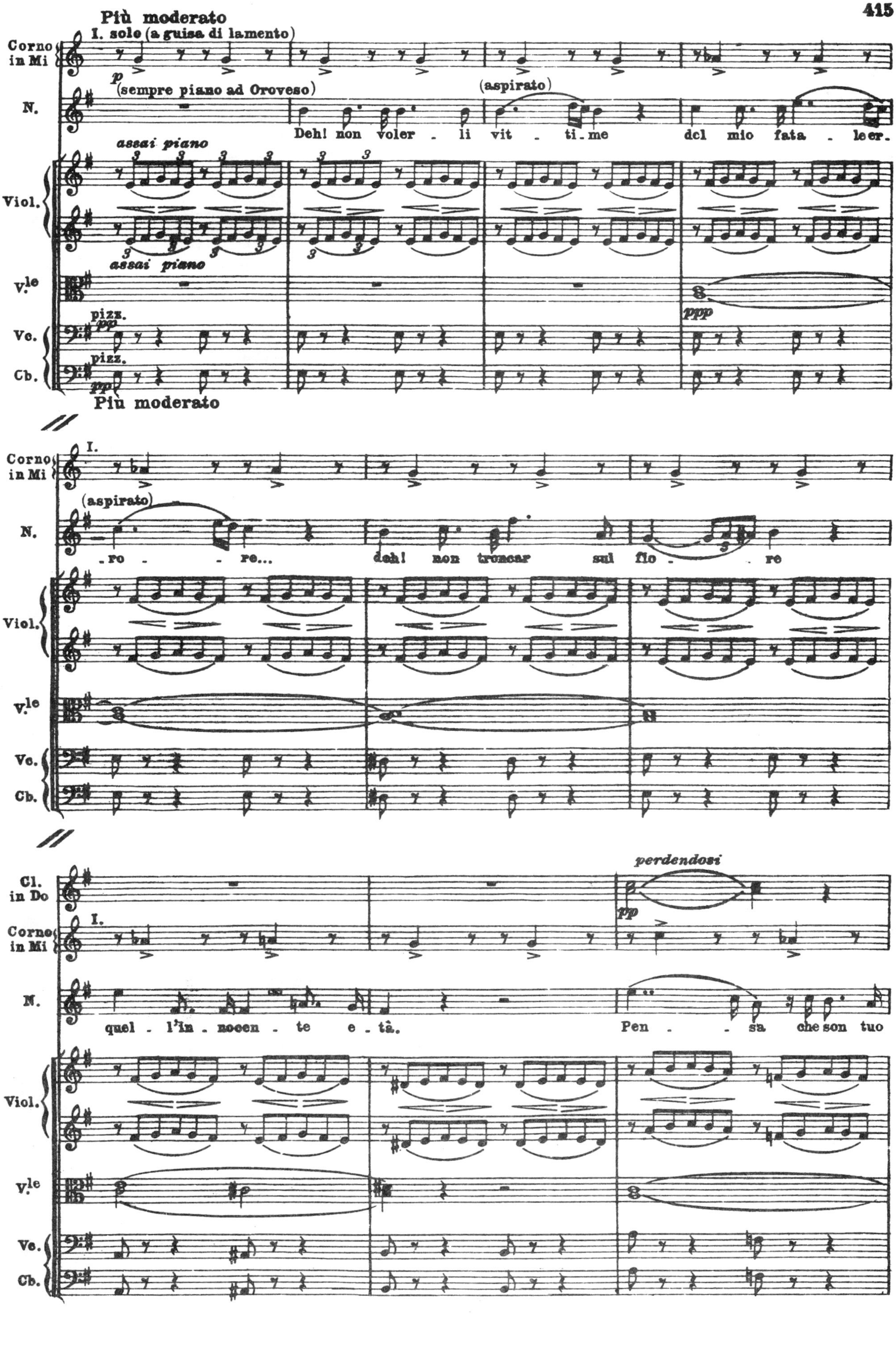

418

424

426

Dover Orchestral Scores

THE SIX BRANDENBURG CONCERTOS AND THE FOUR ORCHESTRAL SUITES IN FULL SCORE, Johann Sebastian Bach. Complete standard Bach-Gesellschaft editions in large, clear format. Study score. 273pp. 9 × 12. 23376-6 Pa. **$11.95**

COMPLETE CONCERTI FOR SOLO KEYBOARD AND ORCHESTRA IN FULL SCORE, Johann Sebastian Bach. Bach's seven complete concerti for solo keyboard and orchestra in full score from the authoritative Bach-Gesellschaft edition. 206pp. 9 × 12. 24929-8 Pa. **$11.95**

THE THREE VIOLIN CONCERTI IN FULL SCORE, Johann Sebastian Bach. Concerto in A Minor, BWV 1041; Concerto in E Major, BWV 1042; and Concerto for Two Violins in D Minor, BWV 1043. Bach-Gesellschaft editions. 64pp. 9⅜ × 12¼. 25124-1 Pa. **$6.95**

GREAT ORGAN CONCERTI, OPP. 4 & 7, IN FULL SCORE, George Frideric Handel. 12 organ concerti composed by great Baroque master are reproduced in full score from the *Deutsche Handelgesellschaft* edition. 138pp. 9⅜ × 12¼. 24462-8 Pa. **$8.95**

COMPLETE CONCERTI GROSSI IN FULL SCORE, George Frideric Handel. Monumental Opus 6 Concerti Grossi, Opus 3 and "Alexander's Feast" Concerti Grossi—19 in all—reproduced from most authoritative edition. 258pp. 9⅜ × 12¼. 24187-4 Pa. **$13.95**

COMPLETE CONCERTI GROSSI IN FULL SCORE, Arcangelo Corelli. All 12 concerti in the famous late nineteenth-century edition prepared by violinist Joseph Joachim and musicologist Friedrich Chrysander. 240pp. 8⅜ × 11¼. 25606-5 Pa. **$12.95**

WATER MUSIC AND MUSIC FOR THE ROYAL FIREWORKS IN FULL SCORE, George Frideric Handel. Full scores of two of the most popular Baroque orchestral works performed today—reprinted from definitive Deutsche Handelgesellschaft edition. Todal of 96pp. 8⅛ × 11. 25070-9 Pa. **$8.95**

LATER SYMPHONIES, Wolfgang Amadeus Mozart. Full orchestral scores to last symphonies (Nos. 35–41) reproduced from definitive Breitkopf & Härtel Complete Works edition. Study score. 285pp. 9 × 12. 23052-X Pa. **$12.95**

17 DIVERTIMENTI FOR VARIOUS INSTRUMENTS, Wolfgang Amadeus Mozart. Sparkling pieces of great vitality and brilliance from 1771–1779; consecutively numbered from 1 to 17. Reproduced from definitive Breitkopf & Härtel Complete Works edition. Study score. 241pp. 9⅜ × 12¼. 23862-8 Pa. **$13.95**

PIANO CONCERTOS NOS. 11–16 IN FULL SCORE, Wolfgang Amadeus Mozart. Authoritative Breitkopf & Härtel edition of six staples of the concerto repertoire, including Mozart's cadenzas for Nos. 12–16. 256pp. 9⅜ × 12¼. 25468-2 Pa. **$12.95**

PIANO CONCERTOS NOS. 17–22, Wolfgang Amadeus Mozart. Six complete piano concertos in full score, with Mozart's own cadenzas for Nos. 17–19. Breitkopf & Härtel edition. Study score. 370pp. 9⅜ × 12¼. 23599-8 Pa. **$16.95**

PIANO CONCERTOS NOS. 23–27, Wolfgang Amadeus Mozart. Mozart's last five piano concertos in full score, plus cadenzas for Nos. 23 and 27, and the Concert Rondo in D Major, K.382. Breitkopf & Härtel edition. Study score. 310pp. 9⅜ × 12¼. 23600-5 Pa. **$13.95**

CONCERTI FOR WIND INSTRUMENTS IN FULL SCORE, Wolfgang Amadeus Mozart. Exceptional volume contains ten pieces for orchestra and wind instruments and includes some of Mozart's finest, most popular music. 272pp. 9⅜ × 12¼. 25228-0 Pa. **$13.95**

THE VIOLIN CONCERTI AND THE SINFONIA CONCERTANTE, K.364, IN FULL SCORE, Wolfgang Amadeus Mozart. All five violin concerti and famed double concerto reproduced from authoritative Breitkopf & Härtel Complete Works Edition. 208pp. 9⅜ × 12¼. 25169-1 Pa. **$12.95**

SYMPHONIES 88–92 IN FULL SCORE: The Haydn Society Edition, Joseph Haydn. Full score of symphonies Nos. 88 through 92. Large, readable noteheads, ample margins for fingerings, etc., and extensive Editor's Commentary. 304pp. 9 × 12. (Available in U.S. only) 24445-8 Pa. **$15.95**

THE MAGIC FLUTE (DIE ZAUBERFLÖTE) IN FULL SCORE, Wolfgang Amadeus Mozart. Authoritative C. F. Peters edition of Mozart's last opera featuring all the spoken dialogue. Translation of German frontmatter. Dramatis personae. List of Numbers. 226pp. 9 × 12. 24783-X Pa. **$12.95**

FOUR SYMPHONIES IN FULL SCORE, Franz Schubert. Schubert's four most popular symphonies: No. 4 in C Minor ("Tragic"); No. 5 in B-flat Major; No. 8 in B Minor ("Unfinished"); and No. 9 in C Major ("Great"). Breitkopf & Härtel edition. Study score. 261pp. 9⅜ × 12¼. 23681-1 Pa. **$13.95**

GREAT OVERTURES IN FULL SCORE, Carl Maria von Weber. Overtures to *Oberon, Der Freischutz, Euryanthe* and *Preciosa* reprinted from authoritative Breitkopf & Härtel editions. 112pp. 9 × 12. 25225-6 Pa. **$9.95**

SYMPHONIES NOS. 1, 2, 3, AND 4 IN FULL SCORE, Ludwig van Beethoven. Republication of H. Litolff edition. 272pp. 9 × 12. 26033-X Pa. **$11.95**

SYMPHONIES NOS. 5, 6 AND 7 IN FULL SCORE, Ludwig van Beethoven. Republication of the H. Litolff edition. 272pp. 9 × 12. 26034-8 Pa. **$11.95**

SYMPHONIES NOS. 8 AND 9 IN FULL SCORE, Ludwig van Beethoven. Republication of the H. Litolff edition. 256pp. 9 × 12. 26035-6 Pa. **$11.95**

SIX GREAT OVERTURES IN FULL SCORE, Ludwig van Beethoven. Six staples of the orchestral repertoire from authoritative Breitkopf & Härtel edition. *Leonore Overtures*, Nos. 1–3; Overtures to *Coriolanus, Egmont, Fidelio*. 288pp. 9 × 12. 24789-9 Pa. **$13.95**

COMPLETE PIANO CONCERTOS IN FULL SCORE, Ludwig van Beethoven. Complete scores of five great Beethoven piano concertos, with all cadenzas as he wrote them, reproduced from authoritative Breitkopf & Härtel edition. New table of contents. 384pp. 9⅜ × 12¼. 24563-2 Pa. **$15.95**

GREAT ROMANTIC VIOLIN CONCERTI IN FULL SCORE, Ludwig van Beethoven, Felix Mendelssohn and Peter Ilyitch Tchaikovsky. The Beethoven Op. 61, Mendelssohn Op. 64 and Tchaikovsky Op. 35 concertos reprinted from the Breitkopf & Härtel editions. 224pp. 9 × 12. 24989-1 Pa. **$12.95**

MAJOR ORCHESTRAL WORKS IN FULL SCORE, Felix Mendelssohn. Generally considered to be Mendelssohn's finest orchestral works, here in one volume are: the complete *Midsummer Night's Dream; Hebrides Overture; Calm Sea and Prosperous Voyage Overture;* Symphony No. 3 in A ("Scottish"); and Symphony No. 4 in A ("Italian"). Breitkopf & Härtel edition. Study score. 406pp. 9 × 12. 23184-4 Pa. **$18.95**

COMPLETE SYMPHONIES, Johannes Brahms. Full orchestral scores. No. 1 in C Minor, Op. 68; No. 2 in D Major, Op. 73; No. 3 in F Major, Op. 90; and No. 4 in E Minor, Op. 98. Reproduced from definitive Vienna Gesellschaft der Musikfreunde edition. Study score. 344pp. 9 × 12. 23053-8 Pa. **$14.95**

Available from your music dealer or write for free Music Catalog to
Dover Publications, Inc., Dept. MUBI, 31 East 2nd Street, Mineola, N.Y. 11501.

Dover Orchestral Scores

THREE ORCHESTRAL WORKS IN FULL SCORE: Academic Festival Overture, Tragic Overture and Variations on a Theme by Joseph Haydn, Johannes Brahms. Reproduced from the authoritative Breitkopf & Härtel edition three of Brahms's great orchestral favorites. Editor's commentary in German and English. 112pp. 9⅜ × 12¼.
24637-X Pa. **$8.95**

COMPLETE CONCERTI IN FULL SCORE, Johannes Brahms. Piano Concertos Nos. 1 and 2; Violin Concerto, Op. 77; Concerto for Violin and Cello, Op. 102. Definitive Breitkopf & Härtel edition. 352pp. 9⅜ × 12¼.
24170-X Pa. **$16.95**

COMPLETE SYMPHONIES IN FULL SCORE, Robert Schumann. No. 1 in B-flat Major, Op. 38 ("Spring"); No. 2 in C Major, Op. 61; No. 3 in E flat Major, Op. 97 ("Rhenish"); and No. 4 in D Minor, Op. 120. Breitkopf & Härtel editions. Study score. 416pp. 9⅜ × 12¼. 24013-4 Pa. **$18.95**

GREAT WORKS FOR PIANO AND ORCHESTRA IN FULL SCORE, Robert Schumann. Collection of three superb pieces for piano and orchestra, including the popular Piano Concerto in A Minor. Breitkopf & Härtel edition. 183pp. 9⅜ × 12¼. 24340-0 Pa. **$10.95**

THE PIANO CONCERTOS IN FULL SCORE, Frédéric Chopin. The authoritative Breitkopf & Härtel full-score edition in one volume of Piano Concertos No. 1 in E Minor and No. 2 in F Minor. 176pp. 9 × 12.
25835-1 Pa. **$10.95**

THE PIANO CONCERTI IN FULL SCORE, Franz Liszt. Available in one volume the Piano Concerto No. 1 in E-flat Major and the Piano Concerto No. 2 in A Major—are among the most studied, recorded and performed of all works for piano and orchestra. 144pp. 9 × 12.
25221-3 Pa. **$8.95**

SYMPHONY NO. 8 IN G MAJOR, OP. 88, SYMPHONY NO. 9 IN E MINOR, OP. 95 ("NEW WORLD") IN FULL SCORE, Antonín Dvořák. Two celebrated symphonies by the great Czech composer, the Eighth and the immensely popular Ninth, "From the New World," in one volume. 272pp. 9 × 12. 24749-X Pa. **$13.95**

FOUR ORCHESTRAL WORKS IN FULL SCORE: Rapsodie Espagnole, Mother Goose Suite, Valses Nobles et Sentimentales, and Pavane for a Dead Princess, Maurice Ravel. Four of Ravel's most popular orchestral works, reprinted from original full-score French editions. 240pp. 9⅜ × 12¼. (Not available in France or Germany)
25962-5 Pa. **$13.95**

DAPHNIS AND CHLOE IN FULL SCORE, Maurice Ravel. Definitive full-score edition of Ravel's rich musical setting of a Greek fable by Longus is reprinted here from the original French edition. 320pp. 9⅜ × 12¼. (Not available in France or Germany) 25826-2 Pa. **$15.95**

THREE GREAT ORCHESTRAL WORKS IN FULL SCORE, Claude Debussy. Three favorites by influential modernist: *Prélude à l'Après-midi d'un Faune, Nocturnes,* and *La Mer.* Reprinted from early French editions. 279pp. 9 × 12. 24441-5 Pa. **$13.95**

SYMPHONY IN D MINOR IN FULL SCORE, César Franck. Superb, authoritative edition of Franck's only symphony, an often-performed and recorded masterwork of late French romantic style. 160pp. 9 × 12.
25373-2 Pa. **$9.95**

THE GREAT WALTZES IN FULL SCORE, Johann Strauss, Jr. Complete scores of eight melodic masterpieces: The Beautiful Blue Danube, Emperor Waltz, Tales of the Vienna Woods, Wiener Blut, four more. Authoritative editions. 336pp. 8⅜ × 11¼. 26009-7 Pa. **$14.95**

FOURTH, FIFTH AND SIXTH SYMPHONIES IN FULL SCORE, Peter Ilyitch Tchaikovsky. Complete orchestral scores of Symphony No. 4 in F Minor, Op. 36; Symphony No. 5 in E Minor, Op. 64; Symphony No. 6 in B Minor, "Pathetique," Op. 74. Study score. Breitkopf & Härtel editions. 480pp. 9⅜ × 12¼. 23861-X Pa. **$19.95**

ROMEO AND JULIET OVERTURE AND CAPRICCIO ITALIEN IN FULL SCORE, Peter Ilyitch Tchaikovsky. Two of Russian master's most popular compositions in high quality, inexpensive reproduction. From authoritative Russian edition. 208pp. 8⅜ × 11¼. 25217-5 Pa. **$10.95**

NUTCRACKER SUITE IN FULL SCORE, Peter Ilyitch Tchaikovsky. Among the most popular ballet pieces ever created—a complete, inexpensive, high-quality score to study and enjoy. 128pp. 9 × 12.
25379-1 Pa. **$9.95**

TONE POEMS, SERIES I: DON JUAN, TOD UND VERKLARUNG, and DON QUIXOTE, Richard Strauss. Three of the most often performed and recorded works in entire orchestral repertoire, reproduced in full score from original editions. Study score. 286pp. 9⅜ × 12¼. (Available in U.S. only) 23754-0 Pa. **$14.95**

TONE POEMS, SERIES II: TILL EULENSPIEGELS LUSTIGE STREICHE, ALSO SPRACH ZARATHUSTRA, and EIN HELDENLEBEN, Richard Strauss. Three important orchestral works including very popular *Till Eulenspiegel's Merry Pranks,* reproduced in full score from original editions. Study score. 315pp. 9⅜ × 12¼. (Available in U.S. only)
23755-9 Pa. **$14.95**

DAS LIED VON DER ERDE IN FULL SCORE, Gustav Mahler. Mahler's masterpiece, a fusion of song and symphony, reprinted from the original 1912 Universal Edition. English translations of song texts. 160pp. 9 × 12. 25657-X Pa. **$9.95**

SYMPHONIES NOS. 1 AND 2 IN FULL SCORE, Gustav Mahler. Unabridged, authoritative Austrian editions of Symphony No. 1 in D Major ("Titan") and Symphony No. 2 in C Minor ("Resurrection"). 384pp. 8⅛ × 11.
25473-9 Pa. **$14.95**

SYMPHONIES NOS. 3 AND 4 IN FULL SCORE, Gustav Mahler. Two brilliantly contrasting masterworks—one scored for a massive ensemble, the other for small orchestra and soloist—reprinted from authoritative Viennese editions. 368pp. 9⅜ × 12¼. 26166-2 Pa. **$16.95**

SYMPHONY NO. 8 IN FULL SCORE, Gustav Mahler. Superb authoritative edition of massive, complex "Symphony of a Thousand." Scored for orchestra, eight solo voices, double chorus, boys' choir and organ. Reprint of Izdatel'stvo "Muzyka," Moscow, edition. Translation of texts. 272pp. 9⅜ × 12¼. 26022-4 Pa. **$12.95**

THE FIREBIRD IN FULL SCORE (Original 1910 Version), Igor Stravinsky. Handsome, inexpensive edition of modern masterpiece, renowned for brilliant orchestration, glowing color. Authoritative Russian edition. 176pp. 9⅜ × 12¼. (Available in U.S. only) 25535-2 Pa. **$10.95**

PETRUSHKA IN FULL SCORE: Original Version, Igor Stravinsky. The definitive full-score edition of Stravinsky's masterful score for the great Ballets Russes 1911 production of *Petrushka.* 160pp. 9⅜ × 12¼. (Available in U.S. only) 25680-4 Pa. **$11.95**

THE RITE OF SPRING IN FULL SCORE, Igor Stravinsky. A reprint of the original full-score edition of the most famous musical work of the 20th century, created as a ballet score for Diaghilev's Ballets Russes. 176pp. 9⅜ × 12¼. (Available in U.S. only) 25857-2 Pa. **$9.95**

Available from your music dealer or write for free Music Catalog to
Dover Publications, Inc., Dept. MUBI, 31 East 2nd Street, Mineola, N.Y. 11501.

Dover Chamber Music Scores

COMPLETE SUITES FOR UNACCOMPANIED CELLO AND SONATAS FOR VIOLA DA GAMBA, Johann Sebastian Bach. Bach-Gesellschaft edition of the six cello suites (BWV 1007–1012) and three sonatas (BWV 1027–1029), commonly played today on the cello. 112pp. 9⅜ × 12¼. 25641-3 Pa. **$8.95**

WORKS FOR VIOLIN, Johann Sebastian Bach. Complete Sonatas and Partitas for Unaccompanied Violin; Six Sonatas for Violin and Clavier. Bach-Gesellschaft edition. 158pp. 9⅜ × 12¼. 23683-8 Pa. **$9.95**

COMPLETE STRING QUARTETS, Wolfgang Amadeus Mozart. Breitkopf & Härtel edition. All 23 string quartets plus alternate slow movement to K.156. Study score. 277pp. 9⅜ × 12¼. 22372-8 Pa. **$13.95**

COMPLETE STRING QUINTETS, Wolfgang Amadeus Mozart. All the standard-instrumentation string quintets, plus String Quintet in C Minor, K.406; Quintet with Horn or Second Cello, K.407; and Clarinet Quintet, K.581. Breitkopf & Härtel edition. Study score. 181pp. 9⅜ × 12¼. 23603-X Pa. **$9.95**

STRING QUARTETS, OPP. 20 and 33, COMPLETE, Joseph Haydn. Complete reproductions of the 12 masterful quartets (six each) of Opp. 20 and 33–in the reliable Eulenburg edition. 272pp. 8⅜ × 11¼. 24852-6 Pa. **$12.95**

STRING QUARTETS, OPP. 42, 50 and 54, Joseph Haydn. Complete reproductions of Op. 42 in D Minor; Op. 50, Nos. 1–6 ("Prussian Quartets") and Op. 54, Nos. 1–3. Reliable Eulenburg edition. 224pp. 8⅜ × 11¼. 24262-5 Pa. **$12.95**

TWELVE STRING QUARTETS, Joseph Haydn. 12 often-performed works: Op. 55, Nos. 1–3 (including *Razor*); Op. 64, Nos. 1–6; Op. 71, Nos. 1–3. Definitive Eulenburg edition. 288pp. 8⅜ × 11¼. 23933-0 Pa. **$13.95**

ELEVEN LATE STRING QUARTETS, Joseph Haydn. Complete reproductions of Op. 74, Nos. 1–3; Op. 76, Nos. 1–6; and Op. 77, Nos. 1 and 2. Definitive Eulenburg edition. Full-size study score. 320pp. 8⅜ × 11¼. 23753-2 Pa. **$13.95**

COMPLETE STRING QUARTETS, Ludwig van Beethoven. Breitkopf & Härtel edition. Six quartets of Opus 18; three quartets of Opus 59; Opera 74, 95, 127, 130, 131, 132, 135 and Grosse Fuge. Study score. 434pp. 9⅜ × 12¼. 22361-2 Pa. **$16.95**

SIX GREAT PIANO TRIOS IN FULL SCORE, Ludwig van Beethoven. Definitive Breitkopf & Härtel edition of Beethoven's Piano Trios Nos. 1–6 including the "Ghost" and the "Archduke." 224pp. 9⅜ × 12¼. 25398-8 Pa. **$11.95**

COMPLETE VIOLIN SONATAS, Ludwig van Beethoven. All ten sonatas including the "Kreutzer" and "Spring" sonatas in the definitive Breitkopf & Härtel edition. 256pp. 9 × 12. 26277-4 Pa. **$13.95**

COMPLETE SONATAS AND VARIATIONS FOR CELLO AND PIANO, Ludwig van Beethoven. All five sonatas and three sets of variations. Reprinted from Breitkopf & Härtel edition. 176pp. 9⅜ × 12¼. 26441-6 Pa. **$10.95**

COMPLETE CHAMBER MUSIC FOR STRINGS, Franz Schubert. Reproduced from famous Breitkopf & Härtel edition: Quintet in C Major (1828), 15 quartets and two trios for violin(s), viola, and violincello. Study score. 348pp. 9 × 12. 21463-X Pa. **$15.95**

CAPRICE VIENNOIS AND OTHER FAVORITE PIECES FOR VIOLIN AND PIANO: With Separate Violin Part, Fritz Kreisler. *Liebesfreud, Liebesleid, Schön Rosmarin, Sicilienne* and *Rigaudon,* more. 64pp. plus slip-in violin part. 9 × 12. (Available in U.S. only) 28489-1 Pa. **$7.95**

COMPLETE CHAMBER MUSIC FOR PIANOFORTE AND STRINGS, Franz Schubert. Breitkopf & Härtel edition. *Trout,* Quartet in F Major, and trios for piano, violin, cello. Study score. 192pp. 9 × 12. 21527-X Pa. **$11.95**

CHAMBER WORKS FOR PIANO AND STRINGS, Felix Mendelssohn. Eleven of the composer's best known works in the genre–duos, trios, quartets and a sextet–reprinted from authoritative Breitkopf & Härtel edition. 384pp. 9⅜ × 12¼. 26117-4 Pa. **$19.95**

COMPLETE CHAMBER MUSIC FOR STRINGS, Felix Mendelssohn. All of Mendelssohn's chamber music: Octet, Two Quintets, Six Quartets, and Four Pieces for String Quartet. (Nothing with piano is included.) Complete works edition (1874–7). Study score. 283pp. 9⅜ × 12¼. 23679-X Pa. **$13.95**

CHAMBER MUSIC OF ROBERT SCHUMANN, edited by Clara Schumann. Superb collection of three trios, four quartets, and piano quintet. Breitkopf & Härtel edition. 288pp. 9⅜ × 12¼. 24101-7 Pa. **$14.95**

COMPLETE SONATAS FOR SOLO INSTRUMENT AND PIANO, Johannes Brahms. All seven sonatas–three for violin, two for cello and two for clarinet (or viola)–reprinted from the authoritative Breitkopf & Härtel edition. 208pp. 9 × 12. 26091-7 Pa. **$12.95**

COMPLETE CHAMBER MUSIC FOR STRINGS AND CLARINET QUINTET, Johannes Brahms. Vienna Gesellschaft der Musikfreunde edition of all quartets, quintets, and sextet without piano. Study edition. 262pp. 8⅜ × 11¼. 21914-3 Pa. **$12.95**

QUINTET AND QUARTETS FOR PIANO AND STRINGS, Johannes Brahms. Full scores of *Quintet in F Minor,* Op. 34; *Quartet in G Minor,* Op. 25; *Quartet in A Major,* Op. 26; *Quartet in C Minor,* Op. 60. Breitkopf & Härtel edition. 298pp. 9 × 12. 24900-X Pa. **$15.95**

COMPLETE PIANO TRIOS, Johannes Brahms. All five piano trios in the definitive Breitkopf & Härtel edition. 288pp. 9 × 12. 25769-X Pa. **$14.95**

CHAMBER WORKS FOR PIANO AND STRINGS, Antonín Dvořák. Society editions of the F Minor and Dumky piano trios, D Major and E-flat Major piano quartets and A Major piano quintet. 352pp. 8⅜ × 11¼. (Available in U.S. only) 25663-4 Pa. **$15.95**

FIVE LATE STRING QUARTETS, Antonín Dvořák. Treasury of Czech master's finest chamber works: Nos. 10, 11, 12, 13, 14. Reliable Simrock editions. 282pp. 8⅛ × 11. 25135-7 Pa. **$12.95**

STRING QUARTETS BY DEBUSSY AND RAVEL/Claude Debussy: Quartet in G Minor, Op. 10/Maurice Ravel: Quartet in F Major, Claude Debussy and Maurice Ravel. Authoritative one-volume edition of two influential masterpieces noted for individuality, delicate and subtle beauties. 112pp. 8⅛ × 11. (Not available in France or Germany) 25231-0 Pa. **$7.95**

GREAT CHAMBER WORKS, César Franck. Four great works: Violin Sonata in A Major, Piano Trio in F-sharp Minor, String Quartet in D Major and Piano Quintet in F Minor. From J. Hamelle, Paris and C. F. Peters, Leipzig editions. 248pp. 9⅜ × 12¼. 26546-3 Pa. **$13.95**

COMPLETE STRING QUARTETS, Peter Ilyitch Tchaikovsky and Alexander Borodin. Tchaikovsky's Quartets Nos. 1–3 and Borodin's Quartets Nos. 1 and 2 reproduced from authoritative editions. 240pp. 8⅜ × 11¼. 28333-X Pa. **$12.95**

---

*Available from your music dealer or write for **free** Music Catalog to*
Dover Publications, Inc., Dept. MUBI, 31 East 2nd Street, Mineola, N.Y. 11501.